NEBRASKA 1994 CHAMPIONSHIP SEASON

Edited By
Suzanne Boggs

Athlon

ACKNOWLEDGMENTS:

Pages 42, 56-58, 60-65, 84, 88-90, 109-110, 118-129 copyright © 1994 The Associated Press. Reprinted with permission of The Associated Press.

Pages 98-99 © copyrighted Chicago Tribune Company. All rights reserved. Used with permission.

Pages 66-69 copyright © 1994 The Dallas Morning News. Reprinted with permission of the Dallas Morning News.

Pages 149-150 copyright © 1995 Fort Myers (Fla.) News-Press. Reprinted with permission.

Pages 39-40, 43-49, 52-53, 65 copyright © 1994 Los Angeles Times. Reprinted with permission.

Pages 145-148, 151-155 copyright © 1995 The Miami Herald. Reprinted with permission.

Pages 41-42, 50-51, 70-72, 86-87, 130-137 copyright © 1994 by The New York Times Company. Reprinted by permission.

Pages 28, 73-83, 138-143 copyright © 1994 The Sporting News. Reprinted with permission.

Pages 27, 30-38, 55, 72, 91, 93-95, 116-117 copyright © 1994 USA TODAY. Reprinted with permission.

Pages 96-97, 100-108, 111-115 copyright © 1994 The Washington Post. Reprinted with permission.

Copyright © 1995 by Athlon Sports Communications Inc.
All Rights Reserved.

No part of this work covered by the copyright hereon may be reproduced or used in any form or by any means—graphic, electronic, or mechanical, including photographing, recording, taping, or information storage and retrieval systems—without written permission of the publisher.

ISBN: 1-886830-00-2

Printed in the United States of America.
First printing.

Edited by Suzanne Boggs.

Book design: Suzanne Boggs
Cover design: Miriam Myers
Photo coordinator: Bill Traughber
Editors: George Leonard, Charlie Miller
Editorial assistants: Alan Ross, William Williams, John Mitchell
Production assistants: Jeralyn Johnson, Jan Jackson, Suzanne Frisina

Published by:
Athlon Sports Communications
220 25th Avenue North, Suite 200
Nashvile, TN 37203

CONTENTS

INTRODUCTION **5**

PRESEASON
Athlon Preseason **18**
A-cademics to Z-atechka **23**

NEBRASKA vs. WEST VIRGINIA (Aug. 28)
Nebraska Nets 31-0 Blowout **27**
Advice to West Virginia: Silence Is Golden **28**
Frazier Opens Heisman Run in Nebraska's 31-0 Victory **30**
Huskers Pound Point Home **32**
Box score and polls **33**

NEBRASKA vs. TEXAS TECH (Sept. 8)
Nebraska Rips Texas Tech 42-16 .... **34**
Box score and polls **38**

NEBRASKA vs. UCLA (Sept. 17)
Will This Be Brawn over Bruins? **39**
Top Two Seeking an Edge in the Polls **41**
A State Dressed in Red **43**
Nebraska Leaves UCLA Seeing Red—In the Mirror **46**
Significant Touchdown at Nebraska **50**
Good News for Bruins Comes Next Season: No Nebraska **52**
Box score and polls **53**
Finding Strength in Numbers **55**

NEBRASKA vs. PACIFIC (Sept. 24)
Pacific No Match for Nebraska **56**
Box score and polls **58**
Nebraska's Frazier Gets OK to Practice **59**

NEBRASKA vs. WYOMING (Oct. 1)
Wyoming Gives Nebraska a Scare, 42-32 .... **60**
Box score and polls **63**
Huskers' Frazier Is Likely Out for Season **64**
Down Goes Frazier, Putting Nebraska's Hopes on Ropes **65**
Nebraska's Frazier Undergoes Surgery **65**

NEBRASKA vs. OKLAHOMA STATE (Oct. 8)
Huskers Win But Lose Another QB **66**
Box score and polls **69**
Nebraska Passers: the Domino Effect **70**
Nebraska Searching for QBs **72**

A Place Like No Other **73**

CONTENTS

NEBRASKA vs. KANSAS STATE (Oct. 15)
Nebraska's Defense Delivers **84**
Kansas State Gets a Dose of Husker Reality **86**
Box score and polls **87**

NEBRASKA vs. MISSOURI (Oct. 22)
Nebraska Avoids New Disasters **88**
Box score and polls **89**
Nebraska-Colorado Stakes High **91**
Phillips Fills Offensive Gap With Big Runs **93**
Nebraska Can't Block Image **96**
QB Berringer bears burden for Huskers **94**
Defense Must Do the Job **98**

NEBRASKA vs. COLORADO (Oct. 29)
Huskers Shred Buffaloes **100**
Buffs Say Cornhuskers Deserve No. 1 .... **109**
Box score and polls **110**
Berringer Gives Huskers Some Breathing Room **111**
Nebraska, Penn St. in a Shoving Match **114**
No. 1 Debate: Polls Provide Split Decision **116**

NEBRASKA vs. KANSAS (Nov. 5)
Campaign for No. 1 .... **118**
Box score and polls **125**

NEBRASKA vs. IOWA STATE (Nov. 12)
Huskers Defeat Iowa St., 28-12 .... **126**
Box score and polls **129**

NEBRASKA vs. OKLAHOMA (Nov. 25)
Nebraska Wins With Offense Below Average **130**
Box score and polls **135**
So Much Perfection. So, Who's the National Champion? .. **136**

The Silent Plainsman **138**

THE ORANGE BOWL: NEBRASKA vs. MIAMI (Jan. 1)
Huskers Making One More OB Run **144**
Huskers Harvest a Dream **145**
Nebraska's Long, Winding Road Has Happy End **149**
Victory Confirms It: Osborne a Champion **151**
Frazier is MVP after Shaky Start **153**
OB Becomes Huskers' Turf **155**
Box score **155**
Team photo and polls **156**
Roster **157**
Final statistics **159**

JOE MIXAN

4

INTRODUCTION

By JEFF KORBELIK
Grand Island Independent

For the University of Nebraska, 1994 national collegiate football champion, the season was a case of unfinished business.

Deprived of the 1993 national title when a last-second field goal against Florida State in last year's Orange Bowl sailed wide left, the Cornhuskers set about making amends. Did they ever! 13-0 and No. 1 in the final polls and *Athlon* rankings after their come-from-behind 24-17 victory over Miami in the Orange Bowl.

"Looking for more in '94" was the team's slogan, the national championship its goal.

"All summer, as we went through conditioning, we felt we had something to prove to the world," said senior linebacker Donta Jones.

Nebraska had its critics. The world doubted coach Tom Osborne's Huskers could pull it off. Teams from the Southeast were touted as the ones to beat.

Athlon picked Miami, Nebraska's Orange Bowl opponent, to win it all. The Associated Press tabbed Florida as did the coaches in the CNN/*USA TODAY* poll. The Huskers were ranked third in August by *Athlon* and CNN/*USA TODAY* in the pre-season and fourth by the AP poll of sportswriters and sportscasters.

1994 saw Nebraska claim its first national championship in 23 years. Star quarterback Tommie Frazier's absence through injury in the final eight regular season games fostered the blooming of Brook Berringer.

INTRODUCTION

Colorado head coach Bill McCartney confers with Nebraska mentor Tom Osborne before the year's most significant Big Eight matchup.

Led by Heisman Trophy candidate Tommie Frazier, Nebraska shut out West Virginia 31-0 in its Kickoff Classic opener in East Rutherford, N.J. The junior quarterback ran for three touchdowns and

threw for another, amassing 230 yards of total offense.

"Tommie made some great plays and some not so good," said Osborne, who has compiled a 219-47-3 record and 11 Big Eight titles in 22 years as head coach; he was an assistant to former coach Bob

Split end Reggie Baul elates after taking a Tommie Frazier pass for a touchdown against West Virginia in the Kickoff Classic. The win placed the Huskers atop the polls.

INTRODUCTION

Devaney when two national championships were won. "But obviously the big advantage we had coming into our first game was at quarterback. He had the experience. He had been there before."

So Frazier was the key.

Gone was Calvin Jones, the powerful Nebraska I-back who opted for the NFL after his junior season.

Brook Berringer huddles the Huskers against conference foe Kansas.

Sideline excitement in Lincoln.

8

INTRODUCTION

A daily reminder challenges the Cornhuskers to the task ahead in '94—nothing less than a national championship.

Tommie Frazier in action against UCLA. One week later Frazier's regular season would end—the result of a blood clot behind his right knee. Fate, however, would return him to glory in the final quarter of the Orange Bowl.

Also gone was 1993 unanimous All-America linebacker Trev Alberts, one of the most decorated defensive players in Nebraska history.

But Frazier was back, and so was his offensive line led by eventual Outland Trophy winner Zach Wiegert and Rob Zatechka, book-end 300-pound tackles.

Nebraska's impressive win convinced the voters. The Huskers vaulted to No. 1.

"So many times, those polls don't make much difference unless they bury you," Osborne said. "The only concern I have is that the fans pay attention to them. They can build up their expectations."

The stay at the top, however, was short, as was Frazier's tenure at quarterback. After the Pacific

INTRODUCTION

game, a blood clot was discovered in his right leg. The injury would sideline him for the rest of the regular season.

Enter Brook Berringer, 6-4 junior backup out of Goodland, Kan. Berringer emerged from Frazier's shadow to lead the Huskers to a 42-32 victory over Wyoming in his first game as a starter. With the Huskers trailing, he guided Nebraska to 21 third-quarter points.

"As far as the team goes, no one expected anything different from me," Berringer said. "The players knew I could play. I knew I could play. I have confidence in my abilities."

Due to their unimpressive win against a team that was 2-2 at the time, the Huskers slipped in the polls, falling behind the explosive Florida Gators.

Nebraska then received more bad news. Berringer was discovered to have a collapsed lung, leaving his availability in doubt for the Oklahoma State game. He played the first half against the Cowboys until another hit deflated the lung again.

Enter Matt Turman, a sophomore walk-on quarterback from Wahoo, Neb. Ahead 9-3 at the half, the Huskers, led by Turman, scored three touchdowns in the final 30 minutes.

Two of those touchdowns came on runs by I-back Lawrence Phillips, who had turned into Nebraska's workhorse after injuries to Frazier and Berringer. The sophomore rushed for a career-high 221 yards against Oklahoma State and would finish the regular season with 1,722 yards (143.5 per game), third-best in the nation.

Husker helmets gleam in the late October sun as Nebraska awaits the kickoff against mighty Colorado.

INTRODUCTION

Lawrence Phillips, the gifted sophomore I-back, would break the Husker season rushing record by a sophomore, held by former Nebraska All-American Bobby Reynolds since 1950, with 1,722 yards.

INTRODUCTION

Would Phillips, Turman and a gimpy Berringer be enough to beat No. 16 Kansas State the next week? Nebraska's defense had an answer to that. The Blackshirts, maligned after the Wyoming game, shut down the Wildcats and quarterback Chad May in a 17-6 win.

"All week long, they were talking a lot of trash in the papers," said Ed Stewart, senior linebacker and Butkus Award finalist. "Talking about how they

Head coach Tom Osborne gives direction to his Huskers on the field during the UCLA game.

Husker horns sound the call to victory.

were going to pick us apart and all that. You can see from the score they didn't do that."

Yet the Huskers' triumph didn't sway pollsters. The AP poll dropped them to No. 3 behind Penn State and Colorado, Nebraska's next big challenge.

INTRODUCTION

Nebraska cheerleaders fire up the Memorial Stadium crowd.

The game with the Buffaloes in Lincoln was do-or-die for both teams. At stake were the Big Eight title, a trip to the Orange Bowl and a possible national championship.

The Huskers made short shrift of the Buffaloes. Berringer completed 12 of 17 passes for 142 yards and a touchdown. Nebraska's defense kept Colorado's Rashaan Salaam, 1994 Heisman Trophy winner, quarterback Kordell Stewart and wide receiver Michael Westbrook in check. And the Huskers prevailed 24-7.

"I hope the voters watched the game," Wiegert, a unanimous All-American, said afterward. "We took on the team that had played the toughest schedule coming in and beat them convincingly."

A week later, the media voted Nebraska No. 1 in the AP poll after Penn State's lackluster performance against Indiana.

Osborne's Huskers would remain on top. No near misses this time, as in 1983 and 1993.

As this coach and this school have persevered for 23 years since Nebraska's last national championship in 1971, Devaney's second straight, this team persevered in the Orange Bowl on the night of Jan. 1, 1995, for three quarters. At that juncture, it trailed Miami by eight points, 17-9. Then, in the fourth period, after wearing down the Hurricanes' defense, the powerful Husker offensive line dominated. Touchdown drives culminated in 15- and 14-yard runs by fullback Cory Schlesinger. And finally a rousing coup de grace by the defense, meted out against Miami's weary, battered offense, completed unfinished business.

16

ATHLON '94 PRESEASON NEBRASKA CORNHUSKERS

Athlon Football 1994

Tom Osborne topped the 200 mark in victories last season, but there's a thorn in his side: He has yet to win the national championship.

That's a burden Osborne until recently shared with friend and coaching rival Bobby Bowden. However, Nebraska's 18-16 loss to Bowden's Florida State Seminoles in the Orange Bowl game was considered by some a springboard to a serious run at the national title in 1994, Osborne's 22nd season as coach of the Cornhuskers.

"I think a number of our players are convinced they can play at that level, and they want to go back and try again," Osborne says.

Nebraska fans have become increasingly postseason-oriented, taking the regular season for granted. Many look to a bowl game as the standard by which to measure their team's success. But Nebraska has lost seven straight bowl games, another burden 206-game winner Osborne carries.

A year ago, Osborne decided a major restructuring was necessary on defense to compete with the nation's best. To that end, he installed a 4-3 base alignment, emphasizing speed and quickness in the manner of Florida State and Miami, recent Nebraska bowl-game nemeses. The change almost accomplished what Osborne hoped for, but a Florida State field goal with 21 seconds to play foiled the Cornhuskers, who finished 11-1.

A year's experience playing under the new philosophy should help offset defensive losses to graduation, notably Butkus Award winner Trev Alberts, a consensus All-American. Offensively, the Cornhuskers continue to work toward an efficient passing component to complement their always potent running game.

Osborne is always most comfortable when he has an experienced quarterback around whom to build his offense, and Tommie Frazier certainly provides that.

Osborne, one of only four active Division I-A coaches with 200 or more victories (Bowden with 239, Penn State's Joe Paterno with 257 and Iowa's Hayden Fry with 200 are the others), laments NCAA legislation limiting recruiting and squad size. Nevertheless, his teams win with consistency. They've won nine or more games in all of his 21 seasons as their coach.

QUARTERBACKS

Frazier is the top returning rusher. The junior ran for 704 yards and nine touchdowns while improving as a passer. He completed nearly 50 percent for 1,159 yards and 12 touchdowns, with only four interceptions. Frazier ranked fourth in the Big Eight in passing efficiency.

Statistics, however, don't measure the qualities that set Frazier apart: competitiveness and heart. That was never more apparent than during Nebraska's 21-17 victory at Colorado, when he returned at the game's end despite the pain of a shoulder strain.

As the Colorado game also showed, as Frazier goes, so go the Cornhuskers. He's the prototypical option quarterback.

Because of the quarterback's injury risks in Nebraska's option offense, depth is important. Osborne will have only two quarterbacks on scholarship behind Frazier, and one will be a true freshman. Junior Brook Berringer, a better pure passer than Frazier, is an experienced backup, but he's bothered by a chronic elbow problem. Sophomore Matt Turman is a walk-on. The other scholarship quarterback is freshman John Elder, who probably will be redshirted.

PRESEASON

◀ Last year, Tommie Frazier completed nearly 50 percent of his passes for 1,159 yards and 12 touchdowns, with only four interceptions.

Junior Tony Veland, a scholarship player, was a quarterback, but he moved to defensive back in the spring and wouldn't return to the offense except in an extreme emergency.

RUNNING BACKS

For the second year in a row, the Cornhuskers have lost a top I-back to the NFL before his collegiate eligibility is complete. This time it was Calvin Jones, last season's leading rusher with 1,043 yards.

Jones' departure left the starting job wide-open. Sophomores Lawrence Phillips and Damon Benning both played in 10 games; Benning started two.

Phillips rushed for 508 yards and five touchdowns. His most notable performances were against UCLA and in the Orange Bowl loss after replacing an ailing Jones. Phillips carried 13 times for 64 yards and a touchdown against the Seminoles.

Unlike Benning, Phillips did not redshirt, evidence of his ability. Osborne says Phillips has the potential to be ranked among the best running backs in recent Cornhusker history.

Among the other I-backs are junior Clinton Childs, sophomore Marvin Sims and transfer Brian Knuckles, who broke former Nebraska All-American Mike Rozier's rushing records at Coffeyville, Kan., Junior College.

Senior Cory Schlesinger is the returning starter at fullback, a position the Cornhuskers are using less these days, with junior Jeff Makovicka as a backup. Makovicka, who played eight-man football in high school, moved from I-back last season and is capable at either position.

RECEIVERS

Senior Abdul Muhammad led the team in pass receptions with 25 for 383 yards and three touchdowns. He was the only receiver with 20 or more catches, though. The ability to block is still a primary requisite for Nebraska's receivers.

Again, Nebraska will have considerable speed but not much size at wide receiver, or tight end for that matter. Among the other returning wide receivers are juniors Reggie Baul, who started one game, and Brett Popplewell, and sophomores Riley Washington and Brendan Holbein.

Washington was considered to have Olympic potential as a sprinter in high school, where he played running back. He's still learning. He caught only one pass last season.

Junior Clester Johnson has played several positions since being recruited as a quarterback. Finally, it appears, he has settled in at wingback, behind Muhammad.

Senior Matt Shaw (6-3, 230) is the most experienced of the tight ends. Senior Eric Alford (6-4, 225), a wingback last season, could line up at tight end, along with junior Mark Gilman (6-3, 240). Shaw didn't catch a pass. Alford and Gilman caught four between them.

Osborne has shown willingness to include running backs in pass patterns as well. Benning was the leading receiver among those returning, with four catches for 27 yards.

OFFENSIVE LINEMEN

Nebraska did not lead the nation in rushing for the first time since 1990. Nor did the Cornhuskers average 300 yards rushing per game. But injuries, more than lack of ability, probably explain that unusual third-place finish.

Hoping to recapture the top spot. Nebraska has the basis for a typically huge, strong line with seniors Zach Wiegart (6-5, 300). Rob Zatechka (6-5, 300) and Brendan Stai (6-4, 300), and junior Aaron Graham (6-4, 280).

Wiegert, a two-time All-Big Eight tackle, should rank among the nation's best. Zatechka, a regular for three seasons, was moved from guard to tackle in the spring. Stai, a guard, is extremely strong. After he was sidelined by a broken fibula seven games into last season, Nebraska's per-game rushing average dropped by more than 40 yards. Graham became the starting center after Stai's injury. He's also the deep snapper. Senior Joel Wilks (6-3, 275) apparently will be the starting left guard.

Among the other returning linemen are seniors Brady Caskey (6-4, 275), Joel Gesky (6-2, 295), Jon Pederson (6-2, 265) and Bill Humphrey (6-2, 260); juniors Steve Ott (6-4, 270) and Bryan Pruitt (6-1, 265); and sophomore Chris Dishman (6-3, 300). Redshirt freshmen Jon Zatechka (6-3, 285), Rob's brother, and Eric Anderson (6-4, 295), could be ready to compete for playing time.

DEFENSIVE LINEMEN

Senior nose tackle Terry Connealy (6-5, 275) was all-conference last season. An eight-man player at a small high school in Nebraska, he has developed into a big-time defender. He'll have to be a key upfront, where experience is lacking, if the Cornhuskers hope to come close to matching 1993, when they ranked first nationally in rushing and first in the Big Eight and 12th nationally in total defense.

None of those alongside Connealy have played a great deal. Christian Peter (6-2, 285), a junior, came on strong at the end of last season, also at nose tackle. He played especially well off the bench against Oklahoma.

Nebraska has little experience at tackle. Senior Jason Pesterfield (6-3, 250), sophomore Larry Townsend (6-4, 300) and Jason Jenkins (6-5, 265), a junior-college transfer who redshirted last season, are among those who could emerge.

Townsend was highly ranked by recruiting analysts out of high school in San Jose, Calif., but he's still learning what it takes to succeed. Once he does, he could be dominating.

Other nose tackles are sophomores Jeff Ogard (6-6, 300) and Scott Saltsman (6-2, 250).

LINEBACKERS

Outside linebacker was a high-profile position because of Alberts and the new defensive alignment. Seniors Donta Jones (6-2, 220) and Dwayne Harris (6-2, 220) head up the 1994 outside linebacker. Jones is in his third full season as a regular, while Harris is just beginning to fulfill the promise he showed when Nebraska recruited him out of Bessemer, Ala.

Harris finished second to Alberts in sacks for the season, with eight for 41 yards in losses. Success in stopping the pass—it ranked first in the Big Eight a year ago—depends on the kind of rush that players like Harris can provide.

Senior Jerad Higman (6-1, 220) and sophomore Ed Morrow (6-5, 225) could see playing time at outside linebacker. Several former redshirts, among them freshman Sean Noster (6-3, 215), could develop on the outside.

Seniors Ed Stewart (6-1, 215) and Troy Dumas (6-3, 220) furnish experience inside. Stewart was among those on whom the switch to a 4-3 was based because of his speed and quickness. He started every game on the weak side.

Others with experience are juniors Doug Colman (6-3, 230) and Phil Ellis (6-2, 220), and sophomore Ryan Terwilliger (6-5, 215). Redshirt freshman Ramone Worthy (6-1, 215), a high school running back, is one of several newcomers who could have an immediate impact at strong-side linebacker.

DEFENSIVE BACKS

With an effective pass rush, the Cornhuskers again should be solid in the secondary. All-Big Eight senior cornerback Barron Miles blocked three kicks, including a punt he recovered for a touchdown in a 27-13 victory at Oklahoma State. Miles also intercepted a pass and broke up five others. Against UCLA, a game Nebraska won 14-13, he was assigned to All-America wide receiver J.J. Stokes and held him to six catches for 65 yards and no touchdowns. Only one other team, Arizona State, kept Stokes from scoring.

Cornerback Kareem Moss and free safety Sedric Collins, both seniors, and sophomores Mike Minter and Eric Stokes are among other defensive backs with experience. Minter was a regular rover back in his first season. Stokes played in 10 games at cornerback, but sat out the Colorado State contest with a knee injury.

The status of junior free safety Tyrone Williams, a returning starter, remains in doubt following off-the-field problems during the off-season.

KICKING GAME

Nebraska ranked first in the Big Eight and sixth nationally in net punting, but punter Byron Bennett has completed his eligibility. Frazier and Miles were listed as backups a year ago, but neither punted. Sophomore Darin Erstad will be among the candidates to punt as well as placekick.

Erstad was an outstanding kicker in high school and will challenge senior placekicker Tom Sieler, who also handled kickoffs last season. Erstad, an outstanding Nebraska baseball player, batted .339, with 10 home runs and 52 RBI, in 1993.

There are plenty of experienced kick returners, among them Baul, Popplewell, Childs, Benning, Moss and the versatile Miles.

However, the Cornhuskers' kick returns were, for the most part, undistinguished last season. That's an area in which there is room for improvement.

ATHLON TOP 25
Preseason Polls

1. Miami
2. Notre Dame
3. Nebraska
4. Michigan
5. Florida State
6. Oklahoma
7. Wisconsin
8. Florida
9. Texas
10. Tennessee
11. Colorado
12. Auburn
13. Stanford
14. Southern Cal
15. Clemson
16. Alabama
17. Penn State
18. Texas A&M
19. UCLA
20. Georgia
21. Arizona
22. Virginia Tech
23. Brigham Young
24. Ohio State
25. Mississippi State

PRESEASON

◀ According to Athlon's 1994 preseason annual, "Zatechka isn't 4.0 on the gridiron yet but he's pretty close."

A-CADEMICS TO Z-ATECHKA

By MIKE BABCOCK
Lincoln Journal-Star

During Nebraska's nine-play, 71-yard drive for a go-ahead field goal in the closing minutes of the 1994 Orange Bowl game against Florida State, 6-foot–5, 305-pound guard Rob Zatechka remained, as always, imperturbable.

Beneath Zatechka's apparently emotionless exterior an "inner fire burned," says center Aaron Graham. However, knowing that didn't help Graham understand his Academic All-American teammate and friend with the perfect 4.0 average. After all, this game was for the national championship.

"Sometimes, I'd look at Rob in the huddle and want to start screaming to see if he was alive," says Graham, one of the most emotional of the Cornhuskers' offensive linemen.

"I don't consider myself to have the ability of the other starters," Graham says, "so I've learned to play with emotion. I don't think you can play football without emotion. With me, it's 80 percent emotion, and 20 percent ability."

If that's the case, Zatechka would be at the opposite end of such a continuum. He is easily the least demonstrative member of Nebraska's offensive line.

As a result of the psychological disparity between these teammates, Zatechka and Graham came to an agreement early last season. Graham would resist the urge to scream at Zatechka, and Zatechka would refrain from trying to calm Graham.

It's a curious arrangement between two of the brightest Cornhuskers.

Zatechka was a GTE/CoSIDA Academic All-American in 1993, with an A average in biological sciences. His goal is medical school and he has applied for a Rhodes scholarship.

Graham earned his academic All-Big Eight honors last season, with a 3.11 grade-point average in animal science. He plans to be a veterinarian.

Nebraska has had 39 GTE/CoSIDA first-team football All-Americans during Tom Osborne's 21 seasons as coach, more than any other major college. Seven have been double winners. And 11 have been offensive linemen, including two-time Outland Award winner Dave Rimington in 1981-82.

Zatechka, a gradate student who will start at left tackle this season, maintained a 4.0 average as an undergraduate, earning all A's. For that matter, Zatechka received straight A's at Lincoln (Neb.) East High School, where he was valedictorian.

"Rob once told me the last B he made was in the second grade," says Graham. "And the weird thing is, I never really see him studying."

In those rare instances when Zatechka makes a mistake on the field, Milt Tenopir, a Nebraska offensive line coach, has used 4.0 to refer to him, according to right tackle Zach Wiegert.

"Coach Tenopir will say, 'How can you have a 4.0 and mess up a football play like that?'" says Wiegert.

"Rob applies things instantly," says Graham. "I'm more of a memorizer. Most people are, I think. The classes he's taking are four times harder than anybody else's.

"Rob can intimidate you two ways. He's huge, plus he can intimidate you with his intelligence. He's somewhere else, above the rest of us mentally."

Studious would describe Zatechka, if he weren't so physically imposing.

Graham is 6-3 and 280, small only by comparison to Zatechka and other returning starters in Nebraska's offensive line: Wiegert (6-5, 300) and guard Brenden Stai (6-4, 300).

Graham says he has drawn inspiration from Zatechka. The two have constantly challenged each other to do well in the classroom. With the considerable demands of playing football at the highest collegiate level and of succeeding academically, there is precious little opportunity to relax.

Zatechka is no egghead, though. He goes out with teammates, has gotten hooked on playing a popular computer football video game and enjoys watching action movies starring Charles Bronson, Chuck Norris and Steven Seagal.

Zatechka may be among the brightest members of the football team, but he's hardly intellectually superior at home. His older brother, Steve, graduated with distinction in Nebraska's honors program and is now in medical school. Jon, Rob's younger brother, is a redshirt freshman offensive lineman for the Cornhuskers. The two could line up alongside each other.

Though Jon's grade-point average isn't 4.0—he got a B-plus in an introductory theater class his first semester as a freshman—it's close. Jon also had straight A's in high school and ranked No. 1 in his graduating class.

Steve Zatechka also had straight A's in high school and was class valedictorian, but he didn't play football.

Rob was the first Cornhusker football recruit to sign a letter of intent in February of 1990. It happened early in the morning at the high school. Jon was a ninth-grader, looking on.

"I remember Jon's face," says Lincoln East athletic director Randy Bates. "He had stars in his eyes."

Four years later, Jon signed a letter of intent with Nebraska.

As is the case with most major college football teams, Nebraska typically watches a movie, as a team, on the night before a game. Two years ago, when the Cornhuskers were upset by Iowa State in Ames, Iowa, they saw the Walt Disney movie, *The Mighty Ducks*.

"It was a nice movie," says Zatechka, "but probably not when you're supposed to be thinking about playing a football game. Ever since, we haven't seen any nice Disney movies before games."

The pregame movies have all been action-packed, which is fine with Zatechka.

"I like a brainless movie," he says. "Anything that doesn't require a lot of thought."

With the Cornhuskers likely to be among the contenders for the national championship again, Graham wishes Zatechka could be just a little more emotional on the field.

"Rob seems to be a monotone the whole time: calm and collected," Graham says. "If we're winning, he's the same as if we're behind. There's never any change in his demeanor."

Zatechka definitely wasn't talking in the huddle when the Cornhuskers made their dramatic drive to take a 16-15 lead against Florida State with 1:16 remaining in the 1994 Orange Bowl game, only to lose 18-16 as time was running out.

"I don't think he's said five words in the huddle in the last three years," Wiegert says.

PRESEASON POLLS

ASSOCIATED PRESS TOP 25

	Team	Rec.	Votes	LS
1.	Florida (15)	11-2-0	1,416	5
2.	Notre Dame (13)	11-1-0	1,414	2
3.	Florida State	12-1-0	1,407	1
4.	Nebraska (18)	11-1-0	1,398	3
5.	Michigan (2)	8-4-0	1,283	21
6.	Miami (1)	9-3-0	1,190	15
7.	Arizona (2)	10-2-0	1,070	10
8.	Colorado	8-3-1	1,057	16
9.	Penn State	10-2-0	1,012	8
10.	Wisconsin	10-1-1	932	6
11.	Auburn	11-0-0	924	4
12.	Alabama (1)	9-3-1	923	14
13.	Tennessee	9-2-1	793	12
14.	UCLA	8-4-0	661	18
15.	Texas A&M	10-2-0	603	9
16.	Oklahoma	9-3-0	560	17
17.	Southern Cal	8-5-0	557	NR
18.	Texas	5-5-1	527	NR
19.	North Carolina	10-3-0	526	19
20.	Ohio St.	10-1-1	320	11
21.	Illinois	5-6-0	249	NR
22.	Virginia Tech	9-3-0	235	22
23.	Washington	7-4-0	181	NR
24.	West Virginia	11-1-0	121	7
25.	Clemson	9-3-0	113	23

USA TODAY/CNN PRESEASON TOP 25

	Team	Rec.	Votes	LS
1.	Florida (17)	11-2	1,416	4
2.	Florida State (13)	12-1	1,402	1
3.	Nebraska (12)	11-1	1,375	3
4.	Notre Dame (12)	11-1	1,362	2
5.	Michigan (3)	8-4	1,302	19
6.	Miami (Fla.) (2)	9-3	1,148	15
7.	Colorado	8-3-1	1,097	16
8.	Arizona (2)	10-2	1,037	9
9.	Penn State (1)	10-2	1,022	7
10.	Alabama	9-3-1	964	13
11.	Wisconsin	10-1-1	902	5
12.	Tennessee	9-2-1	878	11
13.	Oklahoma	9-3	746	14
14.	Southern Cal	8-5	692	25
15.	UCLA	8-4	677	17
16.	Ohio State	10-1-1	644	10
17.	North Carolina	10-3	574	21
18.	Texas	5-5-1	466	NR
19.	Virginia Tech	9-3	301	20
20.	Brigham Young	6-6	281	NR
21.	Clemson	9-3	254	22
22.	Illinois	5-6	249	NR
23.	West Virginia	11-1	209	6
24.	Georgia	5-6	161	NR
25.	Virginia	8-4	138	NR

NEBRASKA NETS 31-0 BLOWOUT

By HARRY BLAUVELT
USA TODAY

EAST RUTHERFORD, N.J., Aug. 28, 1994—Quarterback Tommie Frazier led No. 3 Nebraska to a 31-0 win against No. 23 West Virginia Sunday in Kickoff Classic XII at Giants Stadium.

A junior in his third season as a starter, Frazier scored on runs of 25, 27 and 42 yards. He threw a 12-yard touchdown pass to Reggie Baul.

"I'm surprised we dominated them," said Frazier, the game's most valuable player after running for 130 yards and passing for 100. "I think West Virginia got tired."

It was the third Kickoff Classic win for the Cornhuskers, who previously defeated Penn State (44-6, 1983) and Texas A&M (23-14, 1988).

"This gives us some momentum," Nebraska coach Tom Osborne said.

"Our offense played well, although sporadically, and we can have a great defense."

It was an impressive performance for the Cornhuskers, who amassed a 468-89 advantage in total yards. They limited the Mountaineers, who averaged 233 rushing yards last season, to 8.

"Frazier is really a good player," West Virginia coach Don Nehlen said. "They had the ball so much, our defense just got worn out."

West Virginia, which didn't cross midfield until it recovered a fumble early in the fourth quarter, was shut out for the first time since a 19-0 loss to Penn State in 1986.

Since finishing the 1993 regular season 11-0, West Virginia has lost its last two games by a combined 72-7, including a 41-7 Sugar Bowl setback to Florida.

One of the few West Virginia stars was Todd Sauerbrun, who punted nine times for a Kickoff Classic-record 60.1 average. His 90-yarder in the first quarter was a Kickoff Classic and school mark.

One of Reggie Baul's three receptions was for a touchdown.

Tommie Frazier earned the game's most valuable player award.

ADVICE TO WEST VIRGINIA: SILENCE IS GOLDEN

By IVAN MAISEL
The Sporting News

ST. LOUIS, Mo., Sept. 5, 1994—All right, West Virginia, not a peep out of you for the rest of the season.

The Mountaineers felt as if they had been victimized last season when their 11-0 season went unrewarded with a chance to play for the national championship. They had begun the season so far down in the polls that they couldn't climb all the way to No. 2, much less No. 1.

We refuse to discuss the merits of that case, except to say that justice was served in New Orleans on the night of January 1, when Florida embarrassed the Mountainwhiners, 41-7.

To begin this season, West Virginia had the sporting stage all to itself: The Kickoff Classic, national television on a Sunday afternoon with baseball safely tucked away.

And you thought the Gators embarrassed West Virginia. Nebraska defeated the Mouseketeers, 31-0. The most agonizing thing for West Virginia was that it could have been much worse. The Cornhuskers turned the ball over three times inside West Virginia's 20-yard line and five times overall.

West Virginia finished with 89 total yards, the fewest in Coach Don Nehlen's 15 seasons at the school. The Mountaineers rushed for 8, count 'em, 8 yards, which isn't bad when you consider the Mountaineers began the fourth quarter with minus-16.

Athletic directors like to play in the Kickoff Classic for the $650,000 paycheck. But collecting the money is not without its costs.

"There's a lot of risks, no question about it," Nehlen says, "especially playing Nebraska. We were young and inexperienced. At least we got one game of experience, if nothing else."

West Virginia lost sophomore cornerback Mike Logan with a broken arm. And now the coaches must rehabilitate the psyches of the Mountaineers' quarterbacks. Sophomores Chad Johnston and Eric Boykin proved conclusively that the best quarterback on campus is Major Harris, the former Mountaineers star who is finishing his undergraduate degree.

Nebraska's defense used several blind-side blitzes, so unnerving Johnston and Boykin that they moved out of the pocket in less time than it takes an air bag to inflate. The problem is, neither moved quickly enough to elude the rush. That's how Nebraska finished with eight sacks.

"They were bringing guys off corners and just messing us up," West Virginia guard Tom Robsock said. And he's a senior who made All-Big East last season.

The Mountaineers have lost their last two games by a combined 72-7. They scored the touchdown on their first possession of their loss to Florida in the Sugar Bowl, which means they have played seven-plus scoreless quarters.

There is solace in that Labor Day is upon us. There's time for the Mountainslides to fix what ails them.

Oh, and before we forget, next time you have a chance to watch Tommie Frazier, get him on the tube and toss your channel surfer away.

Tommie Frazier prepares to hand off to Jeff Makovicka under the powerful protection of offensive lineman Brenden Stai.

NEBRASKA VS. WEST VIRGINIA

FRAZIER OPENS HEISMAN RUN IN NEBRASKA'S 31-0 VICTORY

By HARRY BLAUVELT
USA TODAY

EAST RUTHERFORD, N.J., Aug. 28, 1994— Using fancy footwork to frustrate West Virginia, Nebraska quarterback Tommie Frazier took an impressive first step toward the Heisman Trophy Sunday. His performance makes him the early front-runner.

"I'm not worried about the Heisman," Frazier said. "If it comes, I'll be happy. If it doesn't, I'll still be happy if the team is winning."

A veteran at executing coach Tom Osborne's option attack, Frazier ran for TDs of 25, 27 and 42 yards in Nebraska's 31-0 Kickoff Classic XII win. He finished with 130 rushing yards, averaging 10.8 a carry.

"We knew Frazier would be a problem," West Virginia coach Don Nehlen said. "And anytime you can run as well as they do, it's only a matter of time until they throw one over you."

In the second quarter, Frazier tossed a 12-yard scoring pass to Reggie Baul. Frazier completed eight of 16 attempts for 100 yards with two interceptions.

Several of his passes were dropped by Nebraska receivers, including a potential 45-yard TD strike in the second quarter.

"I don't get down on my receivers," Frazier said. "That's all part of the game."

Frazier is a favorite of his massive offensive linemen, who dominated the first half, running 48 plays as the Cornhuskers led 24-0.

"He's easy to block for because you know if you do your job, he'll do his," offensive tackle Zach Wiegert said. "That takes a lot of pressure off."

Against the Mountaineers, Tommie Frazier rushed for 130 yards and three touchdowns, averaging 10.8 yards a carry. His performance vaulted him into the front-runner's position for the Heisman Trophy.

Nehlen compares Frazier to former West Virginia quarterback Major Harris, who led the Mountaineers to an 11-0 record in 1988 before a Fiesta Bowl loss to Notre Dame.

"They're similar, although Major was maybe a little bigger and Frazier is quicker," Nehlen said. "Coach Osborne does the same things with Frazier we did with Major."

Osborne praised Frazier's performance, pointing to his experience as a key in Sunday's game. The Mountaineers played two inexperienced quarterbacks, starter Chad Johnston and Eric Boykin.

"Our offense line controlled the game," Osborne said. "Ask West Virginia's quarterbacks how important that is. It's tough when things are falling in around your ears."

Frazier's ability to run the option kept the Mountaineers off balance most of the sweltering afternoon.

"He's run the option so much, he always knows where the holes are," West Virginia defensive back David Mayfield said. "He doesn't make mistakes. He has great athletic ability and great speed."

As for the Heisman, Frazier would rather talk about his primary focus, finishing first in the polls.

"I never dreamed about winning the Heisman," Frazier said. "What I used to dream about was playing for the national championship."

He realized that goal last January, although Nebraska lost 18-16 to Florida State in the Orange Bowl. "Now, I'd like to win one," he said.

Zach Wiegert fights a defender off of Lawrence Phillips, who ran for 126 yards, 4 yards less than Frazier's total rushing yardage.

HUSKERS POUND POINT HOME

By BRYAN BURWELL
USA TODAY

EAST RUTHERFORD, N.J., Aug. 28, 1994—This was just the sort of football party thick-necked slabs of humanity like Zach Wiegert truly love. This was a body-slamming, smash-mouth feast of drive blocks, pancakes and total steamrolling domination.

Wiegert and all his wide-bodied buddies on the Nebraska offensive line turned steamy Giants Stadium into a theater for the performing art of run blocking in Sunday's 31-0 rout of West Virginia in the Kickoff Classic. It was a well-choreographed chorus line of 300-pound dancing bears pounding the Mountaineers' defensive front to a pulp.

Quarterback Tommie Frazier, the newest Heisman poster boy, slashed all over the place for 130 yards. Tailback Lawrence Phillips slipped and slid through enormous holes for 126 yards. Then it was guys named Jeff Makovicka, Todd Uhlir, Brian Schuster, Damon Benning, Chris Norris and Clinton Childs—four-, five- and six-deep on the Huskers' depth chart—who gallivanted through massive openings created by Wiegert and Co.

But when the game was done, Wiegert was not terribly impressed or needlessly excited. "It was just another game for us," said the 6-5, 300-pound All-America right tackle. "We got a little more work to do."

All those preseason polls look quite nice. All this newfound respect the Huskers earned from their two-point Orange Bowl loss to Florida "The Greatest Team That Ever Lived" State makes them all feel pretty good. Big-mouthed, wisecracking, insulting, cream corn eating jerks like yours truly have all stopped laughing.

The monkey is off their back.

Sort of.

A close loss to Florida State was merely the first step in a treacherous climb back to legitimacy as a national championship contender. Yes, we've all stopped laughing . . . for now.

"Yeah, you know what it's like?" Wiegert said. "It's like the monkey's just standing there waiting to jump back on."

Wiegert chuckled when he said that. He chuckled and nodded his head slowly.

"If we don't go to Texas Tech next week and win big, you guys will be back on us again," Wiegert said. "If we don't win every week—and particularly if we don't win at least one time on Jan. 1—the monkey's right back there."

"People are starting to give us more credit," said senior cornerback Barron Miles.

I know what all you Nebraska lovers are thinking. You're thinking I'm starting it again. The senseless Husker-bashing. The "bowl-impaired" barbs. You're thinking, "This clown was just one missed field goal away from a creamed corn bath, and he's still talking trash."

Actually, I'm trying to show you that even though you might be content with this wave of so-called nationwide respect, the Huskers' players and coaches know it's the football equivalent of a "Miss Congeniality" award.

"Now all of a sudden, people are starting to give us more credit," said senior cornerback Barron Miles. "But it can go away real quick if we don't win on Jan. 1. . . . We know it now. We knew it right after the bowl game (against Florida State). Something wasn't right. Something just didn't feel good."

This "respect" Nebraska is getting from all quarters is not the real thing. It is as flimsy as 100-year-old parchment and fleeting as the next Saturday afternoon defeat.

It is August, surely no time for meaningful discussions about national championships. But here is something worth talking about: Nebraska is seeking something everlasting, the sort of lasting respect that only comes from collecting championship hardware and winning games in January, not August.

Nebraska 31
West Virginia 0

Nebraska.................3   21   0   7 – 31
West Virginia...........0   0   0   0 – 0

Neb—FG Sieler 32
Neb—Frazier 25 run (Sieler kick)
Neb—Baul 12 pass from Frazier (Sieler kick)
Neb—Frazier 27 run (Sieler kick)
Neb—Frazier 42 run (Sieler kick)
Attendance—58,233 (Meadowlands, E. Rutherford, NJ)

TEAM STATISTICS

Category	Neb	W.Va.
First downs	28	9
Rushes-yards	60-368	38-8
Passing yards	100	81
Return yards	152	10
Passes	8-17-2	6-19-2
Punts-Avg.	3-48.3	9-60.1
Fumbles-lost	4-3	4-1
Penalties-yards	6-41	5-44
Time of possession	33:52	26:08

INDIVIDUAL STATISTICS
RUSHING: Nebraska—Frazier 12-130; Phillips 24-126; Schlesinger 8-31; Childs 4-30; Benning 5-19; Makovicka 2-11; Berringer 2-9; Norris 1-5; Uhlir 1-5; Schuster 1-4. West Virginia—Walker 12-46; Barber 6-23; Gary 2-4; Freeman 2-3; Nixon 1-0; Johnston 7-(-29); Boykin 8-(-39).
PASSING: Nebraska—Frazier 8-16-2, 100; Phillips 0-1-0, 0. West Virginia—Johnston 2-6-1, 25; Boykin 4-13-1, 62.
RECEIVING: Nebraska—Baul 3-46; Phillips 2-17; Muhammad 1-23; Gilman 1-7; Holbein 1-7. West Virginia—Vanterpool 3-50; Purnell 2-36; Gary 1-(-5).

ASSOCIATED PRESS TOP 10

	Team	Rec.	Votes	LW
1.	Nebraska (23)	1-0-0	1,465	2
2.	Florida (15)	1-0-0	1,438	1
3.	Notre Dame (10)	1-0-0	1,413	3
4.	Florida State (8)	1-0-0	1,412	4
5.	Miami (Fla.) (1)	1-0-0	1,229	6
6.	Michigan (1)	1-0-0	1,205	5
7.	Colorado	1-0-0	1,140	8
8.	Penn State (1)	1-0-0	1,112	9
9.	Arizona (2)	1-0-0	1,053	7
10.	Wisconsin	0-0-0	968	10

USA TODAY/CNN TOP 25

	Team	Rec.	Votes	LW
1.	Nebraska (20)	1-0	1,463	3
2.	Florida (23)	1-0	1,449	1
3.	Florida State (6)	1-0	1,385	2
4.	Notre Dame (7)	1-0	1,362	4
5.	Michigan (3)	1-0	1,242	5
6.	Miami (Fla.) (2)	1-0	1,209	6
7.	Colorado	1-0	1,138	7
8.	Penn State	1-0	1,128	9
9.	Arizona (1)	1-0	1,024	8
10.	Alabama	1-0	967	10

NEBRASKA RIPS TEXAS TECH 42-16

By OSCAR DIXON
USA TODAY

LUBBOCK, Texas, Sept. 8, 1994—No. 1 Nebraska beat down Texas Tech by the numbers in a 42-16 rout Thursday night.

Nebraska (2-0) rushed for 524 yards.

Lawrence Phillips rushed for 175 yards and two touchdowns.

Tommie Frazier had 172 total yards (84 rushing, 88 passing) and three touchdowns.

The Cornhuskers improved to 68-0 under coach Tom Osborne when rushing for more than 400 yards.

Osborne said his team played well overall but needs a more balanced offensive attack.

"We ran the ball well . . . but we need to throw the ball better."

Frazier, 5-for-15, ran for two touchdowns and threw another. He gave Nebraska an early 7-0 lead with a 58-yard run on the Huskers first possession.

After Texas Tech downed its second-consecutive punt at the Nebraska 2-yard line, the Huskers marched 98 yards on 15 plays to take a 14-0 lead. Frazier capped the drive with his second first-half touchdown, a 3-yard run.

Troy Dumas (4) and Doug Colman (46) helped limit Texas Tech to only 147 yards rushing.

▲ **Lawrence Phillips eludes a Texas Tech defender to score one of his two touchdowns in the game.**

NEBRASKA VS. TEXAS TECH

Cory Schlesinger blocks on special teams as well. Here the Husker fullback wards off the Red Raiders' Duane Price on a Tom Sieler conversion attempt.

The Red Raiders (1-1) got on the scoreboard with 10:43 left in the half on a 49-yard field goal by Jon Davis.

Texas Tech, trailing 14-3 after the first half, took the second-half kickoff and marched 80 yards to cut Nebraska's lead to 14-9. Zebbie Lethridge, who started the second half, hit Scott Aylor with a 6-yard pass with 12:33 to play in the third quarter. The conversion failed.

Nebraska then put together back-to-back 82-yard drives. Cornhuskers fullback Cory Schlesinger picked up 65 of the 82 yards on two carries to set up Phillips' first touchdown, a 2-yard run with 9:01 to play.

The Huskers took a 28-9 lead with 4:19 to play in the third as Phillips raced 56 yards for his second score.

In the fourth quarter, Frazier hit Eric Alford with a 35-yard touchdown pass to give the Cornhuskers a 35-9 with 10:56 left to play.

The Red Raiders scored four minutes later. Darden fumbled at the one, but Ben Kauffman recovered

NEBRASKA VS. TEXAS TECH

Tommie Frazier rushed for two touchdowns and passed for another. On the Huskers' first possession, Frazier ran 58 yards for a touchdown.

Outside linebacker Donta Jones drags down Tech I-back Byron Hanspard, helping hold Tech's total rushing yardage to 147.

37

it in the end zone to bring it to 35-16. Nebraska's Clinton Childs sprinted 30 yards to make the final score 42-16.

Nebraska free safety Mike Minter tore his anterior cruciate ligament in his left knee.

Nebraska 42
Texas Tech 16

Nebraska..................7   7   14   14 – 42
Texas Tech 0   3   6   7 – 16

Neb—Frazier 58 run (Sieler kick)
Neb—Frazier 3 run (Sieler kick)
TT—FG Davis 49
TT—Aylor 6 pass from Lethridge (conversion failed)
Neb—Phillips 2 run (Sieler kick)
Neb—Phillips 56 run (Sieler kick)
Neb—Alford 35 pass from Frazier (Sieler kick)
TT—Kaufman fumble recovery in end zone (Davis kick)
Neb—Childs 30 run (Sieler kick)
Attendance—32,768

TEAM STATISTICS

Category	Neb	TT
First downs	26	17
Rushes-yards	63-524	42-147
Passing yards	88	150
Return yards	5	7
Passes	5-17-1	11-29-1
Punts	3-47	8-41
Fumbles-lost	0-0	1-0
Penalties-yards	5-44	4-30
Time of possession	33:50	26:10

INDIVIDUAL STATISTICS

RUSHING: Nebraska—Phillips 19-175; Schlesinger 6-84; Frazier 13-84; Childs 10-59; Benning 7-45; Schuster 2-37; Makovicka 5-25; Berringer 1-15. Texas Tech—Lethridge 6-62; Crain 15-46; Hanspard 12-27; Darden 7-4; Hobbs 1-7; Walker 1-1.
PASSING: Nebraska—Frazier 5-15-0, 88; Berringer 0-2-1, 0. Texas Tech—Darden 3-10-0, 64; Lethridge 5-14-1, 46; Cavazos 3-5-0, 40.
RECEIVING: Nebraska—Phillips 3-39; Alford 1-35; Baul 1-14. Texas Tech—Scovell 4-74; Mitchell 3-24; DuBuc 2-31; Lavender 1-15; Aylor 1-6.

ASSOCIATED PRESS TOP 25

Team	Rec.	Votes	LW
1. Florida (27)	2-0-0	1,492	2
2. Nebraska (22)	2-0-0	1,483	1
3. Florida State (6)	2-0-0	1,384	4
4. Michigan (2)	2-0-0	1,370	6
5. Miami (Fla.) (1)	2-0-0	1,283	5
6. Penn State	2-0-0	1,239	8
7. Colorado	2-0-0	1,116	7
8. Notre Dame	1-1-0	1,095	3
9. Arizona	2-0-0	1,091	9
10. Wisconsin	1-0-0	1,006	10

USA TODAY/CNN TOP 25

Team	Rec.	Votes	LW
1. Nebraska (34)	2-0	1,501	1
2. Florida (18)	2-0	1,483	2
3. Michigan (5)	2-0	1,383	5
4. Florida State (1)	2-0	1,366	3
5. Penn State (3)	2-0	1,260	8
6. Miami (Fla.) (2)	2-0	1,259	6
7. Colorado (2)	1-0	1,164	7
8. Arizona	2-0	1,060	9
9. Notre Dame	1-1	1,015	4
10. Wisconsin	2-0	1,010	11

WILL THIS BE BRAWN OVER BRUINS?

By JIM HODGES
Los Angeles Times

LINCOLN, Neb., Sept. 17, 1994—Let's see. UCLA is playing No. 2 Nebraska—No. 1 by some counts—and it's here, where the Cornhuskers have won 18 games in a row and the Bruins last won when Coach Terry Donahue was 4 years old.

It's the 196th consecutive sellout, which means 76,000 red shirts worn by people who assume that the Bruins will be served quiche at their pregame meal.

They will be stirred up by the new Diamond Vision, er, Husker Vision screen, and excited about today's home opener for a 2-0 team that has quarterback Tommie Frazier, one of the 767 or so players being touted for the Heisman Trophy. It's also a team that rushed for 527 yards against Texas Tech last week.

Oh, and No. 13 UCLA's best player, All-American wide receiver J.J. Stokes, will be on the sidelines, nursing a thigh bruise.

All those problems, but Donahue claims to have a solution.

"We have a saying, 'When one Bruin goes down, another Bruin takes his place and plays better than he's ever played,'" Donahue said.

Of course, it might not be the right solution.

"We had that saying last week, too, and it didn't generate any big plays," Donahue said.

Nebraska can answer rhetoric with one of college football's most exciting players, Frazier, whose arm is erratic, but who runs the option offense as though his first act as a child was recognizing a crashing defensive end and pitching out to the I-back.

The Cornhuskers also will feature I-back Lawrence Phillips, from Baldwin Park High, who was an unknown quantity until he ran 26 times for 137 yards against the Bruins last year. He is known now, having rushed for 175 yards last week against Texas Tech, working behind a line that is approximately the size of five silos.

▲ Once an "unknown quantity," Lawrence Phillips ran 26 times for 137 yards last year against UCLA.

And Nebraska features a defense that has given up an average of eight points in its two games.

More rhetoric.

"Everybody tries to put them above everybody else," said Stokes. "They're no different than anybody else. Everybody says they can't be beat. Obviously, they can be beat."

They have been beaten once in two years, 18-16, in the 1994 Orange Bowl by national champion Florida State.

Beyond words, though, UCLA has weapons, even if the main one is missing from the four-receiver shotgun offense pirated, perhaps fittingly enough, from Florida State.

"Their two wide receivers, Stokes and [Kevin Jordan] are impressive players and the quarterback, [Wayne] Cook, has good size, throws the ball well and has experience," said Nebraska Coach Tom Osborne before Stokes declared himself unable to play. "So, they'll give us a test, as far as our pass coverage is concerned."

Actually, Cook's experience is in marked contrast to a year ago, when UCLA lost at the Rose Bowl, 14-13.

"I think that's one of the things that will help us," Cook said, "Last year I was playing while looking over my shoulder."

He had just gotten the starting quarterback job and believed his hold on it was tenuous.

"I didn't throw as well as I do now," Cook said. "We stayed with the running game. It was like I wasn't a factor."

He is a factor now, having completed 67.2% of his 67 passes for 499 yards and two touchdowns in leading the Bruins to two victories. Both of the scoring passes went to Jordan, who has 13 receptions for 235 yards.

As important, perhaps, has been the running of Sharmon Shah, who has 291 yards in the best start for a UCLA running back since Freeman McNeil ran for 295 in the first two games of 1979.

"Sometimes they're more dangerous running the ball out of the shotgun than anywhere else," said Osborne. "They've got a lot of clever schemes, and [Shah] really explodes out of there. They've got a lot of ways to hurt you."

And Nebraska has what some call its best team in 25 years.

But how good is it?

Good enough to beat West Virginia, 31-0. Good enough to beat Texas Tech, 42-16. So what?

"This is probably a talent-on-talent situation that will give us a better read on whether we're good or not," Osborne said. "I suspect we're good. I'm sure UCLA is good, so we'll know a little bit more about everything when this is over."

The Bruins may not. They beat a good Tennessee team, 25-23, but struggled against sub-par Southern Methodist before winning, 17-10.

And until Stokes can play—perhaps next week in the Pacific 10 Conference opener against Washington State—it's difficult to gauge the Bruins.

Donahue's fondest wish is to wake up this morning and find that some healing force has Stokes ready to run pass patterns against Nebraska, though he has not practiced in two weeks and said Thursday, "I'll be a spectator."

"To me there's a hope that on game day an athlete wakes up and all of a sudden things change overnight," Donahue said. "There's always a sliver of hope."

He also has occasionally bought lottery tickets.

"I've never gotten more than two numbers, though," Donahue said.

He might well need all six to win at Lincoln today.

TOP TWO SEEKING AN EDGE IN THE POLLS

By MALCOLM MORAN
New York Times

LINCOLN, Neb., Sept. 16, 1994—The bizarre early-season shifts between Nebraska and Florida at the top of the national polls—the unbeaten Cornhuskers and Gators have traded places—may become more clear this weekend. Nebraska will meet U.C.L.A., a team the Huskers defeated by 1 point last season on their way to a perfect regular season, and an opponent that could have an impact on the thoughts of voters.

Not that the polls matter to the coach of the Huskers this early in the season. "I really haven't gone out in the streets and solicited opinions," Tom Osborne said. "I could tell you my reaction is I couldn't care less."

His response might not be shared by the red-clad fans who will produce the 196th consecutive sellout Saturday at the 72,700-seat Memorial Stadium. While the jockeying for position might seem insignificant this early in the season, the order could eventually determine which of the two will play a higher-ranked team to end the season. In the final year of the current arrangement between bowl games, Nebraska and Florida cannot meet to play for a championship.

That arrangement will end next season, when a recently established agreement will rotate a championship game among the Orange, Sugar and Fiesta Bowls. This season, as in recent years, a Nebraska Big Eight Conference championship would place the Huskers in the Orange Bowl. A Florida victory in the Southeastern Conference championship game would send the Gators to the Sugar Bowl.

The combined totals of The Associated Press writers' poll and the USA TODAY/CNN coaches' poll, the figure used by bowl officials to determine post-season matchups, has Nebraska at No. 1 by a 9-point margin over Florida. So Saturday, the Nebraska-U.C.L.A. game, and Florida's encounter

▲ Tony Veland will be taking over for the injured Mike Minter at free safety against UCLA.

at Tennessee, could begin to establish an advantage for one of these top two.

Politically, Nebraska could be hurt when voters take into consideration U.C.L.A. standout split end J.J. Stokes's absence from the lineup Saturday. Stokes has not played since suffering a bruised left thigh in the Bruins' victory over Tennessee on Sept. 3. The absence of Stokes, whose seventh-place finish in Heisman Trophy balloting last year is the highest among returning players, was a factor in U.C.L.A.'s unexpected struggle last week against Southern Methodist.

Stokes is expected to take part in warm-ups Saturday morning, but his status was listed as very doubtful. Two other U.C.L.A. starters will not play: Carl Greenwood, a senior cornerback, and Paul Kennedy, an offensive tackle.

Nebraska has already had to adjust to its own injury problem, with Tony Veland, a former quarterback, replacing Mike Minter at free safety. Veland, who made the first interception of his career in the Huskers' 42-16 victory at Texas Tech, will assume an important role in the defensive scheme. Minter tore a ligament in his left knee at Texas Tech and is expected to miss the rest of the season.

Tommie Frazier, the Nebraska quarterback, was responsible for 3 touchdowns last week to increase his career total to 45–24 passing and 21 rushing. But Frazier completed just 5 of 15, including 1 of his last 9. The offensive balance that Osborne has sought will depend on Frazier's improved consistency and the continued emergence of sophomore I-back Lawrence Phillips.

Phillips ran for 175 yards last week, a total that surpassed his previous career high of 137 last year against the Bruins. "He showed a lot more maturity and a lot more development in the spring," Osborne said. "He shows the potential to rank with some of the better running backs we've had here."

Frazier Hurt

Nebraska quarterback Tommie Frazier remained hospitalized yesterday and continued to undergo tests on his deeply bruised right calf. Frazier was admitted to Bryan Hospital in Lincoln, Neb., on Sunday, one day after No. 2 Nebraska's 70-21 victory over Pacific. The preliminary diagnosis was that Frazier has a vascular problem, Coach Tom Osborne said Sunday, meaning the problem involves his circulatory system. (AP)

A STATE DRESSED IN RED

By ALLAN MALAMUD
Los Angeles Times

LINCOLN, Neb., Sept. 17, 1994—The opponent can be Middle Tennessee State or Oklahoma, the weather a heat wave in September or a snowstorm in November.

No matter what, every Nebraska home football game is a sellout.

Has been since Nov. 3, 1962.

The home opener today against UCLA will be the 196th consecutive full house in Lincoln, an NCAA record.

Memorial Stadium will become the third largest city in the state.

"Wait until you see it," said Brenden Stai, the Cornhuskers' All-American offensive guard from Yorba Linda. "It's awesome, 76,000 people dressed in red and roaring."

Of course, it is the only game in this capital city of 200,000, where the Frisbee was invented and Charles Lindbergh learned to fly.

It is also the only game in a state that does not

Offensive lineman Brenden Stai was recruited by USC and UCLA, but the Husker weight room helped sway him toward Nebraska.

have a major league professional sports franchise.

The same can be said about a number of other states represented by big-time college football teams, but few of them are afflicted with such a fever every fall.

Nebraska football sets attendance records because it is a winner.

A local radio station is conducting a contest that will award "an all-expenses-paid trip for two to Nebraska's bowl game."

Such confidence is justified by the fact that the Huskers—it's Huskers, not Cornhuskers, around here—have been to 25 consecutive bowl games.

A record 26th is a cinch for a team ranked No. 1 in the USA Today/CNN poll and No. 2 in the Associated Press poll.

So what if the Huskers have lost their last seven bowl games?

Coach Tom Osborne, in his 22nd season, has a record of 208-47-3 and ranks either just ahead of or behind Joe Paterno of Penn State in most of the important categories among active Division I-A coaches.

Osborne's reputation is one of the reasons a school that doesn't have the national following of Notre Dame or the in-state recruiting advantages of the Florida schools or Penn State is able to win so consistently.

Stai—who was recruited by UCLA and USC, among others—was asked why he chose Nebraska.

First, he gave the politically correct answer: academics.

Second, the football tradition.

Third, the weight room.

Fourth, the experience of living away from home.

The weight room was the most intriguing.

It isn't really a weight room, it's the Nebraska Strength Complex.

It occupies 30,000 square feet, the largest such facility on any American campus, and is located in a building attached to the south side of the stadium.

"The birthplace for strength and conditioning for collegiate athletes," says the sign in the Strength Complex Museum.

In the lobby are pictures and stories of players selected to the Husker's all-time power team.

There is an offensive team and a defensive team, but, oddly enough, no kicking team.

The teams were selected by strength coach Boyd Epley.

He has six assistant strength coaches and a graduate assistant.

"I started lifting seriously when I was in the 11th grade at Esperanza High," Stai said. "I won a competition there, but I've really been able to improve on my lifts here. This weight room is a diamond."

As a freshman, the 6-foot-4 Stai weighed in at a scrawny 260 pounds.

Now he is a 305-pound senior considered by many NFL scouts to be the best pro prospect in the nation at his position.

Not long ago, he set a Nebraska record by bench pressing 505 pounds.

"The coaches had to kick me out today," he said, grinning after a 45-minute weight session that followed practice on Wednesday. "Some of them think I overdo it, but I don't."

His teammates on the offensive line average 295, and it is no wonder the Huskers play what Stai describes as "smash-mouth football."

They lead the nation with a 446-yard rushing average in their first two games.

The oddsmakers suspect that UCLA will be the latest in the long line of Husker opponents to get smashed in the mouth.

"This game means an awful lot to me," Stai said. "A team from your hometown has to spark some extra excitement in you."

Not that any is needed on a Saturday afternoon in Lincoln in front of 76,000 people dressed in red and roaring.

The Nebraska Strength Complex is touted as "the birthplace for strength and conditioning for collegiate athletes."

NEBRASKA LEAVES UCLA SEEING RED—IN THE MIRROR

By JIM HODGES
Los Angeles Times

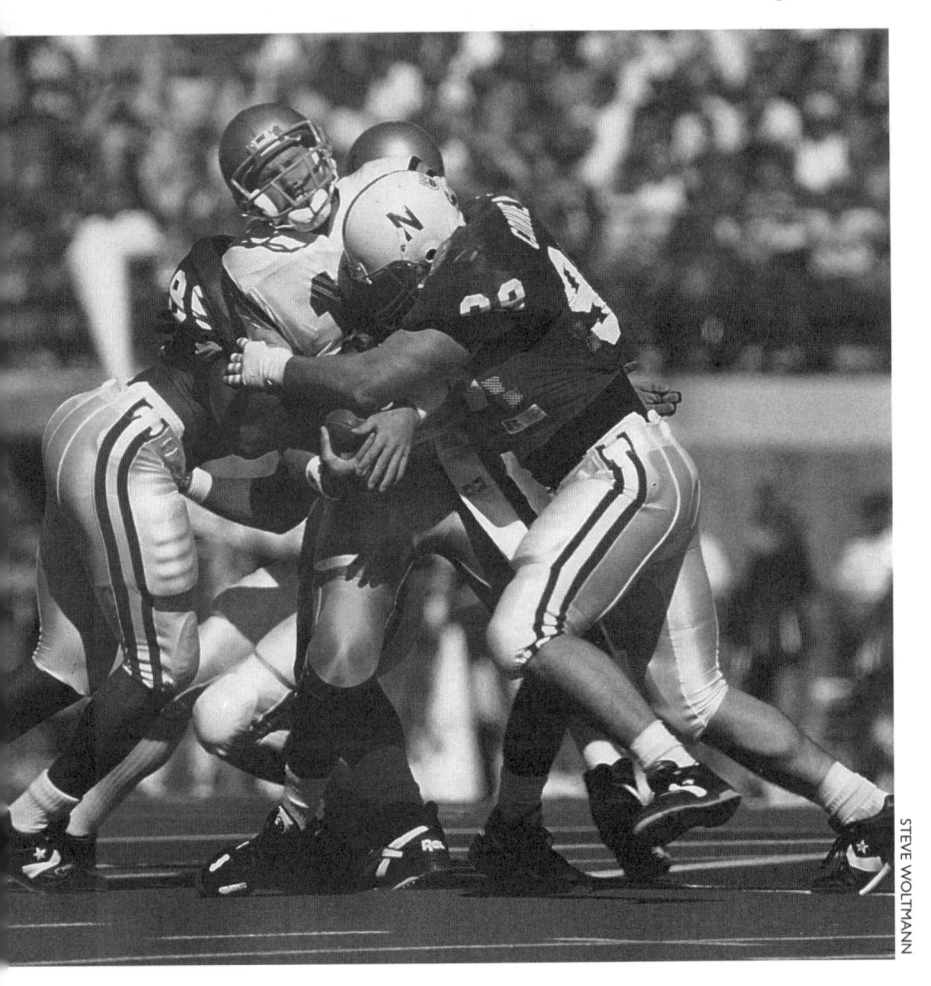

Dwayne Harris and Terry Connealy sack UCLA quarterback Wayne Cook for a loss of 8 yards during a crucial first-quarter drive.

LINCOLN, Neb., Sept. 17, 1994—Nebraska is red cars, red shirts, go Big Red and red hot on offense.

UCLA is red-faced after a 49-21 loss Saturday, and Tommie Frazier is a large part of the reason. Numbers had something to do with it, though most of them weren't his.

"I made the comment before the game that I thought Tommie Frazier was in an elite class of athletes in college football," Bruin Coach Terry Donahue said of the Cornhusker quarterback. "After having played him this year on AstroTurf, I probably feel stronger about my belief than before the game. He's the type of player that makes your whole football team totally different.

"He's a Michael Jordan-type player that just makes a difference in a game."

It wasn't so much that Frazier's numbers were impressive. He carried seven times for 29 yards, scoring one touchdown and two two-point conversions, and he completed only five of 11 passes for 59 yards and two touchdowns.

But he operated Nebraska's option so well that I-back Lawrence Phillips had 178 yards in 19 carries, usually facing only one Bruin after Frazier had strung out the defense, then pitched the ball.

"We established the running game and every running play was working," Frazier said.

The Cornhuskers finished with 484 rushing yards, most against UCLA in what the Bruin record book calls "the modern era," which isn't defined but seems to have something to do with the Great Depression.

"It wasn't so much that he beat us with his athleticism," said UCLA safety Abdul McCullough, who spent much of the afternoon chasing Frazier. "It became a numbers game. He would get to the line of scrimmage and count players on each side of the center. Then he would call 'opposite,' and run the play to the fewest numbers."

It got personal.

"I saw fear in their eyes," Frazier said. "A couple of their linebackers looked like, 'What are they going to run next? And is it going for a big gain?'"

Frequently, it did. And whether the look was fear or respect is open to question.

"The rest of the players are all right," McCullough said. "I mean, Phillips isn't that fast. We've got backs as good as him, but that Frazier dude is the difference."

Tommie Frazier

STEVE WOLTMANN

NEBRASKA VS. UCLA

Eric Alford celebrates the first score of the game, his 23-yard touchdown reception from Tommie Frazier.

STEVE WOLTMANN

He was the difference early, when Nebraska took a 12-0 lead in the first quarter on Frazier's 23-yard touchdown pass to Eric Alford and Phillips' one-yard touchdown run. And he was the difference late, after the Bruins had closed to within 28-14 and Bjorn Merten missed a 42-yard field-goal attempt in the third quarter that would have made it interesting.

Frazier didn't carry on the next series, but he pitched to Phillips on a 60-yard run that included missed tackles by everyone in the secondary. Probably tired, Phillips turned the I-back job over to Clinton Childs for the final eight yards and a 35-14 lead with 2:23 to play in the third quarter.

Childs got his name in the scoring summary, but he knew where the credit went.

"Tommie audibled and ran the option, so they played him, and after I got the ball I knew I had one man to beat [Andy Colbert]. I let him tackle me earlier in the game on a big-play opportunity, so I knew I had to get by him this time, and I did."

Frazier's nine-yard touchdown pass to Brendan Holbein made the score 42-14, and after his 11-yard run on Nebraska's final scoring drive, Frazier called it a day, turning the offense over to Brook Berringer with 12:44 to play.

The Bruins closed to within 49-21 on a Ryan Fien-led drive that covered 85 yards and ended with an 11-yard scoring run by James Milliner with 8:07 to play. It was Fien's first playing time this season, and it began when UCLA quarterback Wayne Cook left the game after being hit on an incomplete pass.

"I just had the wind knocked out of me," Cook said. "I could have come back in. It was a coach's decision."

Cook completed 15 of 28 passes for 217 yards and had a 20-yard touchdown pass to Kevin Jordan. It was the third time the two have hooked up on scoring passes this season, meaning all of Cook's touchdown passes have gone to Jordan.

Cook's four interceptions in the last two games have gone all over the place. Cook had only four all last season, including one in the Rose Bowl, but threw two last week against Southern Methodist that kept the Mustangs close and two more came Saturday in the second quarter.

The first came after Nebraska had taken a 20-7 lead on Frazier's 12-yard option run with 9:34 to play and his two-point conversion run. UCLA was driving, with Sharmon Shah picking up 19 yards and Cook completing passes to Jordan and Daron Washington to the Nebraska 49. Looking for Bryan Adams on a short pass, Cook instead found linebacker Clint Brown, who put the Cornhuskers in business at midfield.

Eight plays later, they were in the end zone, Damon Benning diving over from two yards to end a drive that used the second-string backfield, except for Frazier, who punctuated it by running in for a two-point conversion.

Cook's second interception came when he overthrew Jordan, who apparently missed a pass route adjustment.

"When we go into the game knowing if we give the ball away more than we get it, it's just going to be too hard," Cook said. "We wanted to stay out there and give the defense a break . . . but we couldn't do it.

Instead, he got a chance to be a spectator, watching Frazier and the Nebraska attack.

"Their offense is awesome," Cook said. "If that team is going to get beat, it will be from defense."

That showed when 13th-ranked UCLA (2-1) moved the ball on Nebraska well enough, but mistakes kept the Bruins at bay. Mistakes also are one reason they were embarrassed.

"It's one thing to get beaten if we played our best," tackle Jonathan Ogden said. "It's embarrassing to get beaten like this when we didn't play our best."

Added Cook: "We got our butts kicked. We're embarrassed we lost by so much."

"An embarrassment for us," McCullough said.

Maybe less so today, if Nebraska (3-0) regains the No. 1 spot in the Associated Press poll.

Clinton Childs took over for Lawrence Phillips in the third quarter and quickly made the score 35-14.

SIGNIFICANT TOUCHDOWN AT NEBRASKA

By MALCOLM MORAN
New York Times

LINCOLN, Neb., Sept. 18, 1994—Until last weekend, he was another name on a depth chart, a hard-working sophomore on a team capable of winning a national championship. Brendan Holbein caught one pass last season. This year, as a third-year sophomore, the split end whose college career had begun as a nonscholarship player was making more of a contribution.

On some other Saturday, the first touchdown reception of Holbein's college career would have been a footnote in a game decided long before his most memorable play. Holbein's 9-yard score on a shovel pass from Tommie Frazier was the sixth of seven Nebraska touchdowns in the 49-21 victory over U.C.L.A., an overpowering outcome that still did not prevent the Huskers from losing ground at the top of the combined polls that determine bowl-game matchups.

But after what had happened the previous weekend, after Holbein survived being struck by a stray bullet near the Nebraska campus, one touchdown allowed one sophomore's week to end far better than it had begun. In one small corner of a football-crazed state, for one moment in a bright, happy afternoon, the political maneuverings of the season could be placed aside.

This past weekend was marked by dramatic accomplishments. Florida's 31-0 victory at Tennessee provided two milestones in the Gators' effort to win a first national championship. Florida had not defeated a ranked team on the road in its previous seven attempts under Coach Steve Spurrier. The shutout, Tennessee's worst home defeat since 1924, was a sign of the progress made by the system constructed by new Florida defensive coordinator Bobby Pruett.

Colorado's 55-17 domination of Wisconsin late Saturday, with Rashaan Salaam scoring four touchdowns, became the first of several steps the Buffaloes could take toward championship contention. The next could come in Colorado's game Saturday at Michigan.

Penn State's 61-21 beating of Iowa, in which the Hawkeyes trailed by 42 points before they crossed midfield, increased the anticipation for the meeting between the Nittany Lions and Michigan on Oct. 15. Auburn's three touchdowns in the final 13 minutes, all on interception returns, gave the Tigers a wild 30-26 victory over Louisiana State and extended the nation's longest winning streak to 14 games.

And Alcorn State quarterback Steve McNair threw for 344 yards and two touchdowns and ran for 108 yards in a 39-7 victory over Alabama State. In his three games, McNair has thrown for 1,369 yards and 15 touchdowns.

While all those achievements are considered more significant than an afterthought touchdown as the field at Memorial Stadium here was being covered in a late-afternoon shade, Holbein's moment—his second catch of the day and the fourth of his career—was at least as meaningful.

He was struck from behind on the night of Sept. 9 after an argument developed during a party at an off-campus house rented by two Nebraska players. Holbein, who the police said was a bystander, was hit near his left hip and required 10 stitches. No arrests have been made. Holbein politely declined to discuss specifics of the incident.

Even after the immediate shock had passed, Holbein began to consider how fortunate he had been. "It would be sitting on my mind," he said. "Sometimes I'd be in class and it would be, 'What if it would have been an inch this way, an inch this way?' But as time went on and things started to pass, I knew I had to blank what happened in the past out of my mind."

By Tuesday, the bleeding had finally stopped. By Wednesday, Holbein was back at practice. By Saturday he was part of Nebraska's first home game, on the field for the first offensive series because a formation called for two ends.

"A lot of people said my guardian angel was standing beside me," Holbein said. "I just felt fortunate to be playing today. I'm really happy for that."

By the end of the day, his questions had been answered. "I didn't know how far my extension could go, if I had to catch a deep ball or dive," Holbein said. "I really didn't know if it stretched down there in that area, if I might take a chance on ripping up my stitches."

The stitches had held with the help of extra padding over the wound. An afternoon of collisions did not seem to create any unusual problems. Things seemed back to normal; that is, as normal as Lincoln can be on a football Saturday.

In the combined point totals of The Associated Press writer's poll and the USA Today-CNN poll of coaches, the figure used by the bowl coalition to create the post-season matchups, Nebraska lost 20 points as Florida took over the No. 1 spot. The New York Times computer rankings will kick in soon. The political jockeying between the two could become significant in the final season of the current bowl-game arrangement, because Florida and Nebraska would not be able to meet each other if both teams remain unbeaten.

That was the part of the season that Frazier, the Nebraska quarterback, had in mind when he reviewed the priorities of his teammates. "I think this team has learned a lot from years past," Frazier said. "We can't have problems outside of football."

Until last weekend, Brendan Holbein could not have realized how important his quarterback's observation could be.

Brendan Holbein survived being struck by a stray bullet the weekend before making his first collegiate touchdown reception.

GOOD NEWS FOR BRUINS COMES NEXT SEASON: NO NEBRASKA

By ALLAN MALAMUD
Los Angeles Times

LINCOLN, Neb., Sept. 18, 1994—J.J. Stokes didn't suit up for UCLA Saturday, but Jerry Rice and Sterling Sharpe could have and the Bruins still wouldn't have put much of a scare into Nebraska.

Those people don't play defense.

What the Bruins needed was a Cortez Kennedy in the line, a Ken Norton Jr. at linebacker and a Deion Sanders in the secondary.

Then it might have been close.

The great mismatch on the Great Plains was the Big Red's jumbo, veteran offensive line against the Bruins' undersized, green defense.

Tackle Rob Zatechka, guard Joel Wilks, center Aaron Graham, guard Brenden Stai, tackle Zach Wiegert and tight end Matt Shaw—reading left to right—opened holes big enough for you or me to run through.

Twelve Cornhusker ballcarriers ran for 484 yards, a 7.4-yard average, and five touchdowns.

They improved upon a 446-yard average that had been good enough to lead the nation.

This could be the ninth of Coach Tom Osborne's 22 teams to be crowned NCAA rushing champions.

A fullback, Corey Schlesinger, is averaging nearly eight yards per carry.

His hobby is driving in demolition derbies.

Lawrence Phillips, a sophomore I-back from Baldwin Park, rushed for 178 yards during the 49-21 victory over the Bruins.

He ran 19 times. If Osborne had seen fit, Phillips probably could have run another 19 times for another 178 yards.

Phillips was virtually unstoppable on sweeps.

In other years, some Bruin defensive back about to become a first-round draft pick might have come up and nailed Phillips before he bounded into full flight.

But this time, Coach Terry Donahue started three sophomores and a junior in the secondary.

Oh yes, the Cornhuskers' backfield also includes a bona fide Heisman Trophy candidate.

He is the double-threat quarterback, Tommie Frazier, who passed for two touchdowns, ran for another, and scored a couple of two-point conversions.

Otherwise, his numbers were nothing special.

He passed for only 59 yards.

"We're not looking to make him into Joe Montana," Osborne said.

He ran for only 29, but, make no mistake about it, he is the guy most responsible for keeping Nebraska rivals off balance and guessing.

Among those kept on his heels for much of a clear, 74-degree afternoon was UCLA nose guard George Kase.

"Frazier is the best player we've faced," he said. "He's smart and he reads defenses very well."

Kase, 245, had to try to fight off the surge of a center who weighs 280, guards who weigh 300 and 280, and tackles who weigh 315 and 300.

"They're big, strong and quick," he said. "They beat us up today."

Kase noticed a difference from last year when the Cornhuskers rushed for a total of 208 yards in a 14-13 victory over the Bruins at the Rose Bowl.

"It's a lot different playing them here," he said. "They're so much more intense."

The Cornhuskers put on their game face as early as Friday night.

A crowd estimated at 35,000 roared when the team was introduced during a pep rally that also served to dedicate a couple of new video boards.

On Saturday, the Cornhuskers gave those boards a workout as they scored as many points as any team ever has against Donahue-coached Bruins.

The Big Red was on the verge of scoring at least six more in the closing moments, but the Bruins put on a successful goal-line stand.

Then the strangest thing happened.

As they ran into the tunnel on the way to the dressing room, the visitors were applauded by Nebraska fans in the stands and on the ramps.

They weren't being facetious, either.

Perhaps they have come to feel sorry for the teams who have come to Memorial Stadium since September of 1991 and lost 18 consecutive times.

In the last two weeks on national television, UCLA and USC have been outscored, 87-35, by Nebraska and Penn State.

The defeat was the Bruins' sixth in their last seven games against the Cornhuskers.

"Now we've got Nebraska just where we want them," UCLA Athletic Director Pete Dalis said. "We don't play them next year."

Nebraska 49
UCLA 21

Nebraska.............12   16   7   14 — 49
UCLA....................0   7   7   7 — 21

Neb—Alford 23 pass from Frazier (kick failed)
Neb—Phillips 1 run (pass failed)
UCLA—Jordan 20 pass from Cook (Merten kick)
Neb—Frazier 12 run (Frazier run)
Neb—Benning 2 run (Frazier run)
UCLA—Shah 3 run (Merten kick)
Neb—Childs 8 run (Sieler kick)
Neb—Holbein 9 pass from Frazier (Sieler kick)
Neb—Berringer 1 run (Sieler kick)
UCLA—Milliner 11 run (Merten kick)
A—75,687

TEAM STATISTICS

Category	Neb	UCLA
First downs	31	24
Rushes-yards	65-484	35-129
Passing yards	71	285
Return yards	17	13
Passes	6-12-0	21-35-2
Punts	3-47	4-40
Fumbles-lost	2-1	0-0
Penalties-yards	7-65	4-25
Time of Possession	32:05	27:55

INDIVIDUAL STATISTICS
RUSHING: Nebraska, Phillips 19-178, Childs 7-78, Schlesinger 7-50, Makovicka 7-50, Muhammad 1-30, Frazier 7-29, Benning 8-29, Schuster 2-19, Berringer 2-15, Uhler 2-9, Jackson 1-2, Turman 2-(minus 5). UCLA, Shah 18-91, Milliner 7-38, ayers 4-15, Washington 4-(minus 2), Cook 2-(minus 13).
PASSING: Nebraska, Frazier 5-11-0-59, Berringer 1-1-0-12. UCLA, Cook 15-28-2-217, Fien 6-7-0-68.
RECEIVING: Nebraska, Alford 2-35, Holbein 2-14, Muhammad 1-15, Childs 1-7. UCLA, Jordan 7-129, Washington 4-39, McElroy 2-32, Adams 2-18, Ayers 2-17, Shah 1-20, Anderson 1-14, Nguyen 1-9, Breenan 1-7.

ASSOCIATED PRESS TOP 10

	Team	Rec.	Votes	LW
1.	Florida (33)	3-0-0	1,507	1
2.	Nebraska (20)	3-0-0	1,490	2
3.	Florida State (3)	3-0-0	1,376	3
4.	Michigan (1)	2-0-0	1,336	4
5.	Penn State (1)	3-0-0	1,317	6
6.	Miami (Fla.) (1)	2-0-0	1,262	5
7.	Colorado	2-0-0	1,200	7
8.	Arizona (1)	2-0-0	1,115	9
9.	Notre Dame	2-1-0	1,054	8
10.	Auburn	3-0-0	947	11

USA TODAY/CNN TOP 10

	Team	Rec.	Votes	LW
1.	Nebraska (33)	3-0	1,501	1
2.	Florida (20)	3-0	1,495	2
3.	Florida State	3-0	1,390	4
4.	Michigan (4)	2-0	1,351	3
5.	Penn State (3)	3-0	1,327	5
6.	Miami (Fla.) (2)	2-0	1,242	6
7.	Colorado	2-0	1,201	7
8.	Arizona	2-0	1,100	8
9.	Notre Dame	2-1	1,028	9
10.	Alabama	3-0	1,007	11

Tackle Zach Wiegert opened many of the holes that allowed Nebraska backs to rush for a total of 1,376 yards in their first three games.

FINDING STRENGTH IN NUMBERS

By STEVE WIEBERG
USA TODAY

LINCOLN, Neb., Sept. 19, 1994—Lawrence Phillips was a sprinter on his high school track team. Blink, and he's by you.

Damon Benning and Clinton Childs are a mere tick of the stopwatch slower.

It's a formidable enough collection of talent that Nebraska lines up at tailback this season . . . without the almost three-quarters of a ton of quick-stepping, drive-blocking offensive line in front, carving out running lanes.

"If you can move (the defense) back 2 or 3 yards," coach Tom Osborne says, "our backs are going to find some places to run." Which explains simply and clearly enough how the No. 1-ranked Cornhuskers have left three defenses in succession in absolute tatters.

Vs. West Virginia: 368 yards on the ground.

Vs. Texas Tech: 524 yards.

Vs. UCLA last weekend: 484 yards, including 178 and a touchdown from Phillips.

Four times in the past six years, and a total of eight times under Osborne, Nebraska has won national rushing titles. But the numbers stand out by even that standard.

The Huskers are gaining almost 7 1/2 yards a carry. Their 458.7-a-game average, if it held, would be the second-highest in major-college history, behind Oklahoma's 472.4 yards in 1971.

"Their offense is just overwhelming," UCLA coach Terry Donahue says.

"It was amazing how far downfield their line got," says Bruins linebacker Donnie Edwards, who got in on only three tackles in Saturday's game. "They'd be blocking people 10 yards past the line of scrimmage, and the ball would still be in the backfield."

Of the 'Huskers' 38 All-Americans since Osborne took over the program in 1973, 15 have been offensive linemen. Three have claimed six Outland Trophies and Lombardi Awards as the nation's top linemen.

Tackle Zach Wiegert, a second-team All-American a year ago, is a nominee for a seventh. He and Rhodes Scholarship candidate Rob Zatechka are among four returning starters from the '93 line, with one-time walk-on Joel Wilks stepping into the only vacancy at left guard. Four of the five are fifth-year seniors.

Average height from tackle to tackle: 6-4 1/2. Average weight: 295 pounds.

Yes, they throw that size around. But "there's a little more precision to it than that," Zatechka says. Wiegert was an all-conference basketball player in high school. Wilks played hoops, too. These guys can maneuver.

"They're pretty good athletes for people that big," Osborne says. "A lot of 300-pounders don't have that mobility and ability to change direction."

Amid everything that has gone right this season, Nebraska's passing game is yet to kick in. Quarterback Tommie Frazier, struggling with touch, has completed less than 43% of his attempts for 82 yards a game. "I'm not sure we necessarily have a need to pass," Zatechka says, "But that's something I'd like to see us work on."

The Huskers, meanwhile, have been able to grind out 10 scoring drives of 60 or more yards in their last two games. Phillips, with 479 yards, ranks fifth in the country in rushing as a sophomore, and Childs is averaging 8 yards a carry off the bench.

Frazier, when he has dropped back to pass, has been sacked only once.

Says Osborne: "That offensive line is comforting to have."

PACIFIC NO MATCH FOR NEBRASKA

From The Associated Press

LINCOLN, Neb., September 25, 1994 – The plan was to rest Nebraska quarterback Tommie Frazier, and since the Cornhuskers' opponent Saturday was Pacific, it didn't make any difference.

"Coach [Tom] Osborne told me they didn't want to play me very much," Frazier said after No. 2 Nebraska romped to a 70-21 victory. "I guess 14 points was enough. That's fine with me."

Frazier suffered a leg bruise in last week's 49-21 victory over UCLA and sat out a day of practice early in the week.

Frazier didn't complain about not playing. "It might hurt my stats but we've got enough tough games on the schedule I can prove myself," he said. "I'm not worried about that. There's a long time to go."

Osborne pulled many of his front-line players after the Huskers (4-0) scored quickly in their first two possessions against the outmanned Tigers (2-2). Frazier's backup, junior Brook Berringer, handled things after that, and Nebraska scored on its next five possessions.

▲ Lawrence Phillips leaves the field behind as he sprints 74 yards for a touchdown early in the first quarter.

NEBRASKA VS. PACIFIC

Nebraska's explosive offense was led in scoring by fullback Cory Schlesinger, here scoring one of his two consecutive touchdowns.

Clester Johnson hauls in a 15-yard pass from quarterback Brook Berringer for Nebraska's sixth touchdown, making the score 41-0 in the second quarter.

57

Berringer passed for three touchdowns and ran for another.

"I am very confident," Berringer said after completing eight of 15 passes for 120 yards and rushing six times for 32 yards. "I wanted to go out and show the coaches good poise. I think they do know I have that. And they trust me to go out and play with confidence."

Berringer's 120 yards passing was the best throwing effort by a Nebraska quarterback this season.

"Throwing the ball is probably his best suit," Nebraska quarterback coach Turner Gill said. "But he runs the option well too."

Said Berringer: "I felt pretty good and feel I played well. I had a couple of throws that I wish I had back but overall I felt good. The big key is no turnovers. I was conscious of that and I managed to take care of the ball."

ASSOCIATED PRESS TOP 10

	Team	Rec.	Votes	LW
1.	Florida (31)	3-0-0	1,509	1
2.	Nebraska (22)	4-0-0	1,493	2
3.	Florida State (4)	4-0-0	1,396	3
4.	Penn State (3)	4-0-0	1,369	5
5.	Colorado (1)	3-0-0	1,334	7
6.	Arizona (1)	3-0-0	1,199	8
7.	Michigan	2-1-0	1,145	4
8.	Notre Dame	3-1-0	1,083	9
9.	Auburn	4-0-0	1,008	10
10.	Texas A&M	3-0-0	935	12

USA TODAY/CNN TOP 10

	Team	Rec.	Votes	LW
1.	Nebraska (34)	4-0-0	1,510	1
2.	Florida (22)	3-0-0	1,498	2
3.	Florida State (2)	4-0-0	1,405	3
4.	Penn State (3)	4-0-0	1,373	5
5.	Colorado (1)	3-0-0	1,333	7
6.	Arizona	3-0-0	1,216	8
7.	Notre Dame	3-1-0	1,097	9
8.	Michigan	2-1-0	1,088	4
9.	Alabama	4-0-0	1,061	10
10.	Virginia Tech	4-0-0	894	12

Nebraska 70
Pacific 21

Nebraska	28	21	14	7	— 70
Pacific	0	0	14	7	— 21

Neb—Benning 1 run (Sieler kick)
Neb—Phillips 74 run (Sieler kick)
Neb—Schlesinger 8 run (Sieler kick)
Neb—Schlesinger 39 run (Sieler kick)
Neb—Berringer 6 run (Sieler kick)
Neb—Johnson 15 pass from Berringer (Erstad kick)
Neb—Alford 46 pass from Berringer (Erstad kick)
Neb—Muhammad 18 pass from Berringer (Erstad kick)
Pac—Abdullah 17 pass from Whelihan (Fleenor kick)
Neb—Childs 1 run (Retzlaff kick)
Pac—Abdullah 2 run (Fleenor kick)
Neb—Lake 24 pass from Turman (Retzlaff kick)
Pac—Bowers 9 pass from Sellers (Fleenor kick)
A—75,273.

TEAM STATISTICS

Category	Neb	Pac
First downs	32	20
Rushes-yards	59-510	25-84
Passing yards	189	290
Return yards	94	-2
Passes	12-22-0	27-51-2
Punts	1-45	7-29
Fumbles-lost	2-1	1-0
Penalties-yards	8-90	5-37
Time of possession	31:38	28:22

INDIVIDUAL STATISTICS

RUSHING: Nebraska—Phillips 9-138, Benning 10-87, Childs 10-64, Makovicka 3-59, Schlesinger 3-51, Turman 4-37, Berringer 6-32, Uhlir 3-13, Davenport 2-10, Jackson 2-10, Frazier 1-5, Kucera 1-4, Norris 1-2, Stanley 1-0, Held 1-0, Schuster 2-(minus 2). Pacific—Reeder 4-34, Abdullah 9-20, Green 4-17, Edwards 1-9, Blakney 3-5, Whelihan, 3-0, Wallace 1-(minus 1).

PASSING: Nebraska—Berringer 8-15-0-120, Turman 3-4-0-43, Frazier 1-2-0-26, Kucera 0-1-0-0. Pacific—Whelihan 25-49-2-279, Sellers 2-2-0-11.

RECEIVING: Nebraska—Baul 2-26, Alford 1-46, Childs 1-26, Lake 1-24, Muhammad 1-18, Johnson 1-15, Carpenter 1-12, Holbein 1-8, Vedral 1-7, Benning 1-4, Gilman 1-3. Pacific—Watley 7-126, Brown 4-28, Atkins 4-29, Green 3-26, Morales 2-20, Bowers 2-16, Weston 2-10, Abdullah 1-17, Blakney 1-16, Blackwell 1-2.

NEBRASKA'S FRAZIER GETS OK TO PRACTICE

LINCOLN, Neb., Oct. 1, 1994—Beginning Monday, Nebraska quarterback Tommie Frazier is expected to join the second-ranked Cornhuskers for workouts and could be cleared to play within three weeks, team officials said Friday.

However, Frazier will miss Saturday's game against Wyoming and the Oct. 8 game against Oklahoma State, said sports information director Chris Anderson.

Frazier was released from a Lincoln hospital Wednesday after four days of treatment to dissolve a blood clot behind his right knee. Because he is taking blood-thinners, doctors have banned physical contact because of possible internal injuries or bleeding.

Anderson said if Frazier continues to recover and there is no soreness in his leg, he is expected to be taken off the blood-thinners in about two weeks. That could clear Frazier to play Oct. 15 at Kansas State.

STEVE WOLTMANN

WYOMING GIVES NEBRASKA A SCARE, 42-32

From The Associated Press

LINCOLN, Neb., Oct. 2, 1994—Coach Tom Osborne didn't give No. 2 Nebraska or its coaching staff high grades after the Cornhuskers struggled to a 42-32 victory over Wyoming on Saturday.

"I don't think we played terrible football today, but we can do better than that," Osborne said. "If we don't play better, we're going to have a hard time from here on out."

Lawrence Phillips and backup quarterback Brook Berringer each scored three touchdowns to rally the Cornhuskers from a 21-7 first-half deficit.

Despite the sputtering start, Osborne had praise for his backup quarterback, who made the first start of his career in place of Tommie Frazier, out at least two weeks because of a blood clot in his right leg.

Ironically, Berringer was hospitalized Saturday night with a partially collapsed left lung, according to a broadcast report. Team doctor Pat Clare said Berringer could leave the hospital today and Osborne said the injury did not appear serious and it looks like Berringer will be able to play next week.

Berringer scored on runs of five, 24 and 10 yards and the Cornhuskers (5-0) needed each one to get by Wyoming (2-3).

"I think the Nebraska team probably had to deal with a tremendous amount of distractions this week with the Frazier situation," said Wyoming Coach Joe Tiller.

"And to our credit, we came down and executed well. We had some success, and to their credit, they adjusted to it."

In his first collegiate start, Brook Berringer directed four straight scoring drives in seven minutes to turn a 14-point deficit into a 14-point lead.

NEBRASKA VS. WYOMING

Barron Miles, Nebraska's smallest defensive starter, attempts to block a kick. Miles tallied a pair of interceptions that set up two Husker touchdown drives.

Linebacker Donta Jones puts pressure on Wyoming quarterback Jeremy Dombek, who hit 17 of 35 passes for 264 yards and two touchdowns.

61

NEBRASKA VS. WYOMING

Tight end Mark Gilman attempts to escape the grasp of a Wyoming defender. Gilman had a career-high four receptions for 48 yards.

Linebacker Dwayne Harris (86) prepares to face a Wyoming offense that threatened Nebraska's unbeaten record.

62

Berringer rushed 12 times for 74 yards and completed 15 of 22 passes for 131 yards.

Redshirt freshman quarterback Jeremy Dombek, making his first start for Wyoming, threw a 39-yard touchdown pass to Marcus Harris on the Cowboys' second possession, then found Jeremy Gilstrap from six yards out with 25 seconds left in the first quarter.

Nebraska, using a conservative game plan without Frazier, managed only 58 yards in the first quarter and didn't score until Phillips vaulted in from one yard out with 5:25 remaining in the half.

And Nebraska didn't put the game away until Phillips' eight-yard run following a Wyoming turnover in the fourth period.

Phillips, ranked third nationally, finished with 27 carries and 168 yards in a one-sided duel with the Cowboys' fifth-ranked Ryan Christopherson, who was held to zero net yards in 12 carries.

ASSOCIATED PRESS TOP 10

	Team	Rec.	Votes	LW
1.	Florida (39)	4-0-0	1,521	1
2.	Nebraska (13)	5-0-0	1,449	2
3.	Florida State (4)	4-0-0	1,401	3
4.	Penn State (2)	5-0-0	1,380	4
5.	Colorado (3)	4-0-0	1,355	5
6.	Arizona (1)	4-0-0	1,202	6
7.	Michigan	3-1-0	1,160	7
8.	Notre Dame	4-1-0	1,085	8
9.	Auburn	5-0-0	1,042	9
10.	Texas A&M	4-0-0	957	10

USA TODAY/CNN TOP 10

	Team	Rec.	Votes	LW
1.	Florida (34)	4-0-0	1,516	2
2.	Nebraska (23)	5-0-0	1,485	1
3.	Florida State (1)	4-0-0	1,415	3
4.	Penn State (3)	5-0-0	1,367	4
5.	Colorado (1)	4-0-0	1,333	5
6.	Arizona	4-0-0	1,224	6
7.	Notre Dame	4-1-0	1,132	7
8.	Michigan	3-1-0	1,107	8
9.	Alabama	5-0-0	1,091	9
10.	Miami (Fla.)	3-1-0	959	12

Nebraska 42
Wyoming 32

Nebraska	0	14	21	7	– 42
Wyoming	14	7	3	8	– 32

Wyo—Harris 39 pass from Dombek (Sorenson kick)
Wyo—Gilstrap 6 pass from Dombek (Sorenson kick)
Neb—Phillips 1 run (Sieler kick)
Wyo—Hendricks 1 run (Sorenson kick)
Neb—Berringer 5 run (Sieler kick)
Neb—Berringer 24 run (Sieler kick)
Neb—Phillips 40 run (Sieler kick)
Neb—Berringer 10 run (Sieler kick)
Wyo—FG Sorenson 40
Wyo—Gilstrap 2 pass from Gustin (Gilstrap pass from Gustin)
Neb—Phillips 8 run (Sieler kick)
A—76,234.

TEAM STATISTICS

Category	Neb	Wyo
First downs	24	18
Rushes-yards	56-322	21-36
Passing	131	344
Return yards	53	8
Passes	15-22-1	25-46-3
Punts	8-42	7-41
Fumbles-lost	3-1	2-1
Penalties-yards	9-91	6-30
Time of possession	34:20	25:40

INDIVIDUAL STATISTICS

RUSHING: Nebraska—Phillips 27-168, Berringer 12-74, Benning 6-46, Makovicka 4-19, Childs 3-9, Muhammad 1-3, Schlesinger 3-3. Wyoming—Hendrix 1-33, Gusint 2-9, Dombek 3-7, Hendricks 3-1, Christopherson 12-0.
PASSING: Nebraska—Berringer 15-22-1 131. Wyoming—Dombek 17-35-3 264, Gustin 8-11-80 80.
RECEIVING: Nebraska—Gilman 4-48, Muhammad 4-30, Phillips 3-22, Johnson 2-14, Holbein 1-11, Baul 1-6. Wyoming—Harris 8-149, Pratt 8-126, Gilstrap 3-25, Peace 2-15, Christopherson 2-14, Tillman 1-9, Kuhn 1-6.

HUSKERS' FRAZIER IS LIKELY OUT FOR SEASON

From The Associated Press

LINCOLN, Neb., Oct. 5, 1994—Nebraska quarterback Tommie Frazier, hospitalized with a blood clot in his right leg, is all but certain to miss the rest of the season.

A doctor today recommended surgery and said Frazier, once a leading contender for the Heisman Trophy, should have no physical contact for three to six months.

Dr. Deepak Gangahar, a cardiovascular surgeon, said the 20-year-old junior from Bradenton, Fla., should remain in the hospital for a week to 10 days for an operation.

Gangahar, speaking at Bryan Memorial Hospital, told Coach Tom Osborne of his recommendation regarding the restrictions. Osborne, at practice with the No. 2 Cornhuskers (5-0), was not immediately available for comment.

"Medicine is an inexact science," Gangahar said. "But as it goes today that is my recommendation to the coach."

He said Frazier showed no expression when told the news.

"Tommie kept his chin up and recognized the reality," Gangahar said.

The doctor said he is 90 percent sure Frazier will have surgery to tie off a surface vein that had a smaller blood clot. That smaller vein, he said, likely rubbed against the larger inner vein, causing the second blood clot in two weeks.

The larger second clot discovered Tuesday has been dissolved, Gangahar said. Doctors now want Frazier's blood to gradually thicken so they can operate to tie off the smaller vein.

After a first clot, about 6 to 8 inches long, was discovered Sept. 25 behind Frazier's right knee, Gangahar said Frazier would be out for the season if the clot formed again.

While clots like Frazier's are not rare, Gangahar said they usually occur in elderly patients or those stricken with heart disease or cancer.

"We have done numerous tests to determine that he is not suffering from any other blood or disease related problems," he said.

Frazier was spending "some private time with his mother," said Chris Anderson, the university's sports information director. Priscilla Frazier of Bradenton, Fla., came to Lincoln today.

"She said she wanted to spend some time with her son and would not be talking to reporters," Anderson said.

Gangahar said Frazier had complained of a sore calf before the Huskers' victory over U.C.L.A. on Sept. 17. However, neither Frazier nor Osborne could determine when Frazier might have taken a hit to the leg.

Having the second clot appear without further trauma and while Frazier was on blood thinner complicated the situation, Gangahar said. That's why doctors had to explore other causes.

Although he never redshirted, Frazier is unlikely to regain a year of eligibility for medical hardship if he misses the rest of the season.

"It appears that he has played in too many games this season to be eligible for the hardship status," said Al Papik, Nebraska's N.C.A.A. compliance officer.

Nebraska could seek a waiver of the rules for special consideration because of extenuating circumstances, Papik said.

DOWN GOES FRAZIER, PUTTING NEBRASKA'S HOPES ON ROPES

By GENE WOJCIECHOWSKI
Los Angeles Times

LINCOLN, Neb., Oct. 6, 1994—Had everything gone as planned—and it hasn't for poor Nebraska quarterback Tommie Frazier—the Cornhusker star would have sat out Saturday's game against Oklahoma State, maybe would have played the next week against Kansas State and most definitely would have started against Missouri Oct. 22.

"If nothing unusual develops," Nebraska Coach Tom Osborne had said.

But then came the news Tuesday that Frazier had developed a second blood clot in his right leg, once again requiring hospitalization. On Wednesday, a doctor recommended surgery and said Frazier should have no physical contact for three to six months, meaning he is lost for the season.

A full recovery, of course, is what matters most.

But the fact remains that Nebraska is a significantly less dangerous team without Frazier in the lineup. Nothing against backup Brook Berringer, who is recovering from a partially collapsed left lung (he's fine now; no rib damage was discovered), but Nebraska can't beat Colorado Oct. 29 in Lincoln without Frazier.

Berringer, who was hurt despite wearing a football flak jacket, scored three touchdowns in a 10-point victory against Wyoming last Saturday, but that's the problem—it was against Wyoming, now 2-3.

Of course, don't tell Osborne that.

"It was one of the most brutal games I've been around in a long time," he said of the hard hitting.

Berringer, who spent last Saturday night and then Sunday in the hospital, is back at practice and is expected to start against Oklahoma State . . . and Kansas State . . . and every other game remaining on the schedule.

And pity the Cornhuskers if Berringer goes down. Two of Nebraska's best prospects, scholarship quarterbacks Ben Rutz and Jon Elder, transferred to other schools in the last year because they didn't want to wait for playing time. That leaves Osborne with the following choices: 1) Berringer; 2) non-scholarship player Matt Turman, a sophomore; 3) safety Tony Veland, a former quarterback switched to defense early in the 1993 season; 4) walk-on Monte Christo, who is recovering from hand surgery; 5) Adam Kucera, a former team trainer; 6) Ryan Held, a converted wide receiver; 7) retirement.

Nebraska's Frazier Undergoes Surgery

From The Associated Press

LINCOLN, Neb., Oct. 7, 1994—Tommie Frazier underwent surgery Thursday for recurring blood clots in his right leg, but the star Nebraska quarterback is still almost certain to sit out the rest of the season.

Doctors at Bryan Memorial Hospital in Lincoln tied off a vein believed to be contributing to the clots. Deepak Gangahar, a cardiovascular surgeon, said the operation went well.

Frazier, 20, a junior from Bradenton, Fla., should remain in the hospital for a week to 10 days and avoid physical contact for three to six months, Gangahar said.

Playing contact sports while on blood thinners would be dangerous because of the risk of internal bleeding if there is an injury.

Meanwhile, doctors continued to monitor backup quarterback Brook Berringer, who sustained a partially collapsed lung last week but is scheduled to start for No. 2 Nebraska against Oklahoma State on Saturday. He will wear a protective pad for extra protection.

HUSKERS WIN BUT LOSE ANOTHER QB

By STEVE RICHARDSON
Dallas Morning News

LINCOLN, Neb., Oct. 8, 1994—Second-ranked Nebraska's quarterback shuffle continued Saturday in a 32-3 victory over Oklahoma State. The uncertainty of who might start against 19th-ranked Kansas State next Saturday lingered long after the Cornhuskers' 21st straight victory over the Cowboys.

"Maybe we will have auditions Monday," said Nebraska coach Tom Osborne in a rare show of humor.

Walk-on Matt Turman took over at quarterback for Brook Berringer in the second half, and quickly won the approval of Husker fans by leading the team to victory.

The Cornhuskers (6-0) wound up with seldom-used sophomore Matt Turman at quarterback throughout the second half, mostly for handoffs and runs. In the first half, starter Brook Berringer suffered a partially collapsed lung.

Berringer, a junior, was taken to the Student Health Center at halftime for X-rays, which proved positive. For the second straight week, Berringer's left lung had to be inflated after collapsing 30-40 percent.

"I was hit with about six-seven minutes left in the first half," Berringer said. "I knew I was in trouble when I got in the squad car (bound for the Health Center)."

Berringer, who said he believes he can play Saturday in Manhattan, Kan., had made his first career start a week earlier in place of Heisman Trophy candidate Tommy Frazier. Berringer played all the way in a 42-32 victory over Wyoming.

Frazier, the Nebraska starter the first four games, was declared out for the season Wednesday because of recurring blood clots in his right leg.

Will Berringer be able to play against Kansas State (4-0) or make it through an entire game? Osborne hinted he may have two defensive backs, junior Tony Veland and senior Barron Miles, both of whom have played quarterback during their careers, ready to take snaps. He said he will let Nebraska doctors decide whether Berringer can play.

"We're going to work out a way to make it, no matter who plays where," Osborne said. "So we'll get the thing put back together."

Despite the Cornhuskers' continuing quarterback problems, the Cowboys (3-2) were no match for them Saturday before a sellout crowd of 75,453 at Memorial Stadium. Lawrence Phillips had career highs in rushes (33) and yards (221) while scoring three touchdowns. And the Cornhuskers'

NEBRASKA VS. OKLAHOMA STATE

▶ At halftime, X-rays proved that Brook Berringer had suffered a collapsed left lung for the second straight week.

NEBRASKA VS. OKLAHOMA STATE

Lawrence Phillips dives into the end zone for one of his three touchdown runs. Phillips also had career highs in rushes (33) and yards (221).

Although Oklahoma State was the first to put points on the board, Nebraska defenders like Christian Peter made sure those three points were the last by limiting the Cowboys to 136 yards total offense.

defense limited Oklahoma State to 136 yards total offense.

"I think they have got some struggles at quarterback," Oklahoma State coach Pat Jones said. "But they've still got an awfully good supporting cast. Their defense will have to turn it up."

Nebraska led only 9-3 at halftime after the offense sputtered behind Berringer. And the second half could have been a disaster for Nebraska.

Turman, a walk-on from Wahoo, Neb., who has yet to earn a scholarship, attempted only four passes and completed one, not counting a successful two-point conversion throw. He gained six yards on six rushes.

"I think we played pretty well in the second half," Turman said. "We scored three touchdowns in the second half. And we won. That's the bottom line."

Nebraska 32
Oklahoma St. 3

Nebraska	0	9	16	7	— 32
Oklahoma St.	3	0	0	0	— 3

OSU—FG Vaughn 27
Neb—Phillips 2 run (kick failed)
Neb—FG Erstad 48
Neb—Phillips 2 run (Alford pass from Turman)
Neb—Phillips 7 run (Erstad pass from Vedral)
Neb—Childs 7 run (Erstad kick)
A—75,453.

TEAM STATISTICS

Category	Neb	OSU
First downs	30	7
Rushes-yards	68-372	31-40
Passing yards	103	96
Return yards	68	5
Passes	12-20-0	6-20-1
Punts	2-34	9-41
Fumbles-lost	4-3	2-1
Penalties-yards	5-49	3-31
Time of possession	36:55	23:05

INDIVIDUAL STATISTICS
RUSHING: Nebraska—Phillips 33-221, Childs 6-45, Benning 7-42. Oklahoma St.—Thompson 11-35, Jefferson 5-15, Richardson 6-8.
PASSING: Nebraska—Berringer 10-15-0-75, Turman 1-4-0-23, Vedral 1-1-0-5. Oklahoma St.—T. Jones 6-20-1-96.
RECEIVING: Nebraska—Muhammad 4-53, Childs 2-22, Baul 2-5, Benning 1-7, Holbein 1-6, Gilman 1-5, Makovicka 1-5. Oklahoma St.—D. Jones 2-33, Denson 1-34, Thompson 1-15, Watts 1-11, Richardson 1-3.

ASSOCIATED PRESS TOP 10

	Team	Rec.	Votes	LW
1.	Florida (44)	5-0-0	1,527	1
2.	Nebraska (12)	6-0-0	1,461	2
3.	Penn State (4)	5-0-0	1,427	4
4.	Colorado (4)	5-0-0	1,410	5
5.	Michigan	4-1-0	1,251	7
6.	Auburn	6-0-0	1,193	9
7.	Texas A&M	5-0-0	1,106	10
8.	Miami (Fla.)	4-1-0	1,104	13
9.	Washington	4-1-0	1,072	12
10.	Alabama	6-0-0	1,022	11

USA TODAY/CNN TOP 10

	Team	Rec.	Votes	LW
1.	Florida (43)	5-0-0	1,527	1
2.	Nebraska (13)	6-0-0	1,479	2
3.	Penn State (5)	5-0-0	1,417	4
4.	Colorado (1)	5-0-0	1,387	5
5.	Michigan (1)	4-1-0	1,247	8
6.	Alabama	6-0-0	1,193	9
7.	Miami (Fla.)	4-1-0	1,171	9
8.	Florida State	4-1-0	1,050	3
9.	Texas	4-1-0	927	15
10.	Arizona	4-1-0	903	6

NEBRASKA PASSERS: THE DOMINO EFFECT

By WILLIAM C. RHODEN
New York Times

LINCOLN, Neb., Oct. 13, 1994—The players say they can't remember anything like it. Tom Osborne says he has never seen anything like it in 22 years of coaching at Nebraska.

As undefeated Nebraska goes into a critical Big Eight game against Kansas State, the Cornhuskers find themselves with a quarterback quandary of major proportions. After starting the season with a Heisman Trophy candidate, the Huskers may be down to a walk-on when they take the field in Manhattan, Kan., Saturday against what is certain to be a fired-up Kansas State team and crowd.

The domino effect began with Tommie Frazier, the Cornhusker quarterback who was off to a Heisman-type year, on Sept. 25, when a blood clot was diagnosed in a vein just above his right knee. The clot was dissolved two days later, but Frazier was readmitted on Oct. 4 when a second blood clot appeared in the same spot. He had surgery on Oct. 6 and was released on Tuesday, but he is out for the season.

Enter Brook Berringer. Replacing Frazier, he made his first career start against Wyoming Oct. 1, but the 6-foot-4-inch junior suffered a collapsed lung in the first half after being sandwiched between two tacklers while scoring one of three touchdowns. Berringer suffered the same injury a week later against Oklahoma State. This time he missed the entire second half. Berringer practiced on Wednesday and today, but his status won't be determined until Saturday.

That brings Matt Turman into the picture. Turman is a 5-11, 165-pound walk-on from Wahoo, Neb. Before the rash of injuries thrust him into prominence, Turman's claim to fame before last week was that his uncle was married to Osborne's wife's sister.

Now he's facing the game of his life. Kansas State is rated first in The New York Times computer rankings, 11th in the USA Today/CNN poll and 16th in The Associated Press ranking. Nebraska is ranked fourth by The Times and second in each of the other polls.

"I never dreamed anything like this would ever happen," Turman said.

Neither did Osborne. The injuries to Frazier and Berringer have created a bizarre chain reaction. A walk-on potentially becomes the starter; a wide receiver, Clester Johnson, is backing up the walk-on at quarterback, and a former student manager, 5-8 Adam Kucera, suddenly seemed elevated into the quarterback chain. Well, maybe not. Osborne announced Wednesday night that Kucera had banged up his shoulder.

Saturday's game marks Nebraska's first appearance at Kansas State since 1990, when Nebraska won by 45-8. The Wildcats have not beaten Nebraska since 1968 when they won, 12-0, at Nebraska, and have not beaten Nebraska at home since 1959. This is the Wildcats' "Everything Bowl."

"I think they're probably licking their chops," said Turman, who played for his father at Neumann High in Wahoo. "That suits me fine. I'm going to get out there just like anybody else and get the ball moving and I'm going to do what has to be done."

Playing in place of Berringer, Turman led the Cornhuskers to three second-half touchdowns in a 32-3 victory over Oklahoma State last Saturday.

To think that three years ago Turman was about to leave Nebraska and transfer to a smaller school where he could play, and probably start, at quarterback. His father convinced him to stay. "He told

THE QUARTERBACKS

Tommie Frazier: Heisman Trophy candidate turned sideline cheerleader.

71

me to give it a shot because if you don't it's something you'll always wonder about if you don't," Turman said.

For Berringer, Frazier's injury provided the answer to a question: "Will I ever have a chance to lead this team?" He and Frazier are both juniors and before the injury, Frazier was improving each game. Berringer was beginning to wonder.

"Any time you're a backup things go through your mind," he said. "I was content with where I was, but I was excited about the opportunity to start and show what I could do."

Johnson may be the most excited Husker of all. As a backup wide receiver, Johnson, 5-11 and 210 pounds, has played in every game this season. But Saturday's game may mark the first time since high school he's taken a snap from center.

An All-State quarterback at West High in Bellevue, Neb., Johnson came to Nebraska with the idea of being a quarterback. He switched to defense—playing in the secondary briefly—when the line at quarterback became too long. In addition to Frazier and Berringer, Johnson discovered that there were "six or seven" other quarterbacks.

He switched to offense in 1992, moving to receiver, but has never lost the desire to play quarterback.

Monday he learned he was in the rotation.

"We had a big team meeting and Coach Osborne announced that I would take some snaps," Johnson said. "I didn't jump up and scream but I smiled to myself."

After a tentative start on Monday, Johnson felt more comfortable on Tuesday. By Wednesday he was convinced he could run the offense if necessary. "It all came back to me," he said, smiling. "The feeling of standing in front of the huddle, calling the plays, having the ball.

"If Brook gets hurt and Matt's moving the ball, I don't see me coming into the game. But if coach feels I can do a better job I'll be happy to go in there. I can get things done. If I got in there I may surprise a couple people who never got a chance to see what I could do."

Nebraska Searching for QBs
USA Today
Oct. 12, 1994

WANTED: Quarterback for nationally ranked college football team. Experience not required. Call University of Nebraska, ask for Tom.

That want ad hasn't appeared in Nebraska newspapers yet, but coach Tom Osborne has been having auditions. Going into Saturday's game against No. 11 Kansas State (4-0), quarterback Tommie Frazier is probably out for the season with recurring blood clots in his right calf.

Backup Brook Berringer suffered a partially collapsed left lung in Nebraska's 42-32 win against Wyoming Oct. 1 and might be unavailable for Kansas State. No. 3 quarterback Matt Turman will play Saturday if Berringer can't. Backing up Turman—second-team wingback Clester Johnson, who last played quarterback three years ago.

Johnson was recruited as a quarterback, but the junior moved to defensive back and then wingback his first season. At least he's on offense, which means he deals with the same plays every day, Osborne said.

That isn't the case for safety Tony Veland and cornerback Barron Miles, who have also been taking snaps at quarterback.

A PLACE LIKE NO OTHER

By TERRY FREI
The Sporting News

HYANNIS, Neb., population 210, is 320 miles northwest of our red-drenched football weekend in Lincoln. Yet because Nebraska football involves exceptional statewide devotion to a single Division I-A program, it's not inappropriate to start with the reconstructed scene at Hyannis High on a Friday night in early October.

At the high school on the east edge of town— past the Grant County courthouse, the Dyer Feed Store and Dredla's Grocery and the Sandhill Oil filling station—the Hyannis Longhorns are about to kick off under the lights against the Hay Springs Hawks in eight-man football. Already, a few of the Hyannis fans are wearing white T-shirts commemorating the weekend and a favorite son, Nebraska senior defensive tackle Terry Connealy. The creases still are crisp, the iron-on logos pristine. Hyannis, so often overlooked by selective atlas publishers, is the *only* dot on this shirt's Nebraska map. Connealy's name is in block letters. His number—99—is superimposed across Nebraska, stretching from South Dakota into Kansas. The message: HOMETOWN PROUD!

The Bank of Hyannis bought 250 tickets to the Nebraska-Oklahoma State game, printed the T-shirts honoring Connealy, the Cornhuskers' Outland Trophy contender, then sold the tickets and shirts at cost to residents of Hyannis and surrounding Grant County (population 767). Some Hyannis fans are making it a doubleheader: The Longhorns on Friday night, then the Huskers vs. Oklahoma State the next day. Others are skipping the high school game and already have left for Lincoln. By Saturday, Hyannis, never bustling, will be all but deserted. Virtually everybody will be in Lincoln, showing off those T-shirts and honoring Connealy on his "Senior Day."

Coincidentally, the travelers from Hyannis will be part of the Cornhuskers' 199th consecutive sellout. That NCAA-record streak began in 1962, when Memorial Stadium's capacity was 31,080. It has lasted through expansion and some non-league home breathers for the '80s and '90s against the Utah States and Northern Illinoises of the Division I-A world. The Huskers' "soft" non-league schedule at times has been exaggerated; they have played quality non-league opponents and also have had to fill in scheduling holes when other opponents dropped out. The sellout streak will reach 200 Saturday, when more than 75,000 will fill the frequently expanded erector set of a stadium for the game against the Colorado Buffaloes. The *hated* Colorado Buffaloes.

To the residents of Hyannis and the other towns of northwest Nebraska, it is irrelevant that they are closer to the Colorado campus than to Lincoln, or that they tend to be fans of the Denver Broncos and other Colorado professional franchises. If you live within the borders of Nebraska, the Huskers are your major college team. Your only team. And the hell with everyone else.

On this Friday night, the Hyannis Longhorns get started on what will be a 32-28 victory over Hay Springs.

In Lincoln, Terry Connealy and most of his Nebraska teammates are on the game-eve team outing, viewing the start of "The Specialist" at the Plaza 4. The Huskers are the No. 2 team in the polls, but Coach Tom Osborne and his team have a problem: As they watch Sharon Stone and Sly Stallone steam up the screen, the Huskers' quarterback—Tommie Frazier—is recuperating in Bryan Memorial Hospital after undergoing surgery earlier in the week to combat blood clots in his right leg. Frazier is going to be all right, but he probably is lost for the season; and now the Huskers have one remaining scholarship quarterback, untested junior Brook Berringer. He's backed up by Matt Turman, a 5-foot-11 walk-on sophomore from Wahoo, Neb. Turman looks more like the kid who should be taking tickets at the Plaza 4 door than a quarterback for a national-championship contender.

They'll worry about that later.

Bill Byrne's year-old house is adjacent to the country club on Lincoln's east side. He has been the athletic director at Nebraska since 1992, and his hiring was a tough sell. There were in-house candidates, and Byrne—the successful and respected A.D. at Oregon—was an outsider. But he seems to have won over the Nebraska loyalists, and he now is trying to shepherd through a plan to build skyboxes at Memorial Stadium, again expanding the capacity and giving the athletic department a significant new source of revenue.

Even when you're selling out for decades, the financial pressures are immense. So on the night before Sellout No. 199, Byrne isn't being merely the gracious A.D./host as he and his wife, Marilyn, put on a dinner party and serve the best salmon that can be flown into Nebraska. Some of the Huskers' boosters are present, mingling among the athletic department staff, plus guests from Oklahoma State, Jim Barker of the Orange Bowl committee and the two-man contingent from *The Sporting News*.

Byrne and his staff earlier had recommended a couple of stops on our itinerary of game-weekend discovery. Like everyone else, they had these wry little smiles when they brought up the Sidetrack Tavern. By all means, they said, we had to take in the show at the Sidetrack. They said they wouldn't try to explain it; we'd just have to see it. The Sidetrack? At Byrne's house, the woman from the catering service says, conspiratorially: "That's where I'd be if I weren't working."

First, however, we stop at Misty's restaurant, Lincoln's slightly more wholesome Friday night tradition for both Nebraska and visiting fans. The restaurant serves a cut of prime rib some offensive linemen can't finish. The display case in the waiting area has helmets from every Division I-A program in the nation. Sports banners and the logos of all Big Eight schools are on the walls. The bar in the bustling lounge is shaped like a football, and a gold statue of Jerry Tagge, quarterback of the 1971 national championship team, rotates over the shelves of liquor stock.

At 9, right on time, 13 members of the Cornhuskers' marching band strut down the stairs, belting out the fight song. They're wearing white tux

Terry Connealy—the pride and joy of Hyannis, Nebraska.

shirts and red bow ties. After parading through the eating area—diners put down their forks to stand and clap—they adjourn to a stage in the lounge. For the next 30 minutes, they put on a mini-pep rally and concert. A contingent of Husker yell leaders (Nebraskan for "cheerleaders") leads cheers. One poor girl stands on the shoulders of a yell king, and she has to be careful not to scrape the ceiling with her fingernails. After a couple of renditions of the fight song, and even a quick rendition of the Oklahoma State fight song, the band marches back to a meeting room. Elvis has not left the building; he's just taking a break. The second set is at 11.

Jay Hoffman, 23, is in his third year in the Friday night band and is the leader for the season. He says the Misty's assignments go "to the committed group. These people have been in band three or four years and this is kind of their reward."

A senior economics major, Hoffman is a Lincoln native. "You can't grow up here and not know about the Friday night tradition," he says. "It's not like you live here and there's a football team. It's you live here and you're part of the football team, part of the tradition.

"When you play for the Colorado game or the Oklahoma game, it's absolutely nuts around here. Of course, they're hammered beyond belief. The crowd is pumped up, it's standing room only wall to wall."

But isn't this a combustible mixture, especially when the Big Eight rivals come to town? Alcohol, rivalries, the band playing both fight songs? What about this newly virulent rivalry with the *hated* Colorado Buffaloes?

"We don't talk about the Colorado fans," Hoffman says. "They're pretty much a bunch of whiners. They come out here and think it's going to be a Colorado pep rally. It's like, 'Wake up, this is Nebraska, this is our pep rally.' We say, 'Yeah, we'll play your stupid fight song, but . . . ' They're a bunch of whiners. If you get them hammered enough, though, they'll pay you 20 bucks every time you play their fight song." He smiles. "I guess there's something good to say about Colorado fans."

Bob Milton, the owner of Misty's and the newer Misty's II (which doesn't have a Friday night show), says the game-eve tradition began back in the late 1960s. "I got acquainted with Bob Devaney," he says of the former Huskers coach and athletic director, who by now is probably on dessert at Byrne's house. "He brought a lot of football players out here. He'd bring recruits. At that time, you could hire football players to gladhand people, to shake hands and wear red sportcoats. Now you can't do that. But I stayed involved."

Many of the visiting teams have their Friday night squad dinner in a Misty's meeting room. Oklahoma does it every time. The *hated* Colorado Buffaloes do not.

At the Sigma Nu fraternity on 16th Street, the party is just getting started. Fraternities officially are dry at Nebraska. Wink.

Connealy and the Huskers are bused back to the Nebraska Center, the on-campus hotel where they stay the nights before home games. Connealy is counting them down—three home games left in his career, starting with Oklahoma State the next afternoon.

His father, Marty, is a sandhills rancher, a former Nebraska scholarship player who didn't play a down because of a heart murmur. Marty has had season tickets since 1968 and is the president of the Big Red Cattle Club, which annually donates "a beef" to be auctioned off to benefit the athletic development fund. Marty's brothers, Jerry and

Jack, played for the Huskers in the 1970s.

At Sellout No. 87, when the Huskers met Alabama on September 17, 1977, Terry's name was on the Memorial Stadium public-address system for the first time. He was 5. "They announced: 'Marty Connealy, you're lost and your son Terry is looking for you at gate so and so,'" Marty says.

Terry was a multi-sport athlete at little Hyannis High. "I never let him know that there was any place other than Lincoln to go to college," his father says.

Says the 6-5, 275-pound Terry: "As long as I can remember, it's been an obsession. I think every little boy in Nebraska wants to play Nebraska football. I never took any other official trips. I did go to Wyoming for a few games"—again, Hyannis is far closer to Laramie than Lincoln—"and I was talking to some other schools. But I committed early, and after I committed, I didn't take any trips anywhere else."

With its population of about 1.6 million, Nebraska doesn't have nearly enough in-state prospects to produce a perennial national-championship contender. The Cornhuskers and the *hated* Colorado Buffaloes are among the national leaders in states represented: This season, the Huskers list players from 31 states, the *hated* Buffaloes from 21 states, the District of Columbia, Canada and Samoa. Of the Huskers' 22 position starters against Oklahoma State, three each come from California and New Jersey; and one apiece come from Texas, Kansas, Alabama, Maryland, South Carolina, Illinois, Wyoming and Florida. That leaves eight starters from Nebraska, including Connealy; and over the years, a surprising number of Huskers' regulars have come from within the borders.

Both in terms of recruiting and financial resources, the Huskers clearly benefit from the single-program obsession, which makes you wonder what it would be like if such relatively lightly populated states such as New Mexico and Oregon, and perhaps even Kansas and Iowa, mustered all their Division I-A football energies behind one program. The attraction for out-of-staters is winning and being the focal point of not merely the campus, but of an entire state.

Tommie Frazier came to Lincoln from Bradenton, Fla.

Before tightened scholarship limits, Nebraska was among the most adept in the nation at stockpiling scholarship and walk-on players. One quarterback goes down? Eight other guys step forward and contend for the job. Now? With Frazier out and Brook Berringer still affected by a lung problem, the concern is that while the Huskers can overpower Oklahoma State with the waterboy at quarterback, they might have problems down the road. Against Kansas State, for example. And/or against the *hated* Colorado Buffaloes. The QB

In the first start of his career, Brook Berringer managed to lead the Huskers to a win over Wyoming, but his injuries have some fans concerned about upcoming games with Kansas State and Colorado.

BRIAN JACKSON

issue is one reason the first question to the TSN contingent from the band at Misty's was not when this story was going to run, but: "What do you think of Berringer?" They're thinking ahead, to Kansas State the next week, and especially to Colorado. Even on this night in early October, the odds seem good that by the time that Colorado game arrives, both teams still will be undefeated, the stakes will be the Big Eight title and continued national championship contention and the national press will have flocked to Lincoln and asked Osborne for the 1,373rd time if he won't feel complete as a head coach until one of his teams has finished No. 1.

With Tommie Frazier out of the picture, Tom Osborne must find another way to take his Nebraska team to their first national title.

It's coming up to curfew at the Nebraska Center. Terry Connealy's family already has settled in at the Airport Inn, where they've had a standing game-weekend reservation for 26 years. Chris Kraus, the Hyannis High coach, is savoring the victory over Hay Springs and is on the highway, hoping to make it to Kearney for a few hours sleep and then to get up early to finish the drive to Lincoln. And at the Sidetrack Tavern, they're just getting rolling.

Sidetrack Tavern owner Joyce Durand looks matronly but has a voice that can peel paint and a vocabulary that would make a hockey player blush. She doubles as the piano player in the house band at the Sidetrack, a cavernous, cacophonous warehouse that is packed and raucous most nights, downright riotous the night before a game. The band has no name, and Joyce is joined by Paul Newton and Fred Meyer.

Occasionally—oh, no more often than once every 11 minutes—the band breaks into the Nebraska fight song and gets the crowd *really* going.

"There is no place like Nebraska

"Dear old Nebraska U. . . ."

The rest of the time? Students and others in the mixed-age crowd hand Durand notes on napkins, and she reads them all, especially those from self-proclaimed "Sidetrack virgins" and those that make obscene references to the opponents and media.

Then we're hearing familiar tunes, many of them adapted for the football crowd, with rewritten lyrics so vile, filthy and disgusting I know the Sidetrack folks will be proud to have that proclaimed in a national publication. Newton writes most of the lyrics, and one song is an obscene biological suggestion for ESPN commentator Craig James, who apparently is anathema for life in Lincoln because he knocked the Huskers last season.

(Hey, Joyce, just ask Craig, the former Southern Methodist running back, how many games his alma mater has won since the Mustangs had to institute a salary cap.)

(Sorry, Craig. That's a real cheap shot. Guess Lincoln just rubs off.)

The Sidetrack songs and banter-filled interludes from the musicians include barbs directed at just about every college football media personality, network and publication in the country. In Lincoln, you see, they still don't think the Huskers get enough of what Aretha Franklin sang about. That's such a pervasive lament in athletics nowadays, I refuse to even use the word; but in Lincoln, the virulence is striking . . . but also funny.

The other big hit of the night is Durand's "I love/I hate" song. Guess which applies to "Coach Bill McCartney and the Colorado Buffaloes?" She describes her affection or contempt in words that largely shall have to go unreported, but when someone in the audience tosses a paper missile at the stage, Durand says: "You keep throwing stuff like that, people might think you're from Colorado!"

Newton introduces a parody to the tune of Billy Joel's "The Longest Time" with this admonition to TSN over the microphone: "Feel free to reprint this song, but only in its entirety." Entirety? We can't even get in an entire line.

By now, I'm thinking: And I told the gang back at TSN this was going to be about the most wholesome college football weekend experience in America. But I'm shaking my head, saying this is just awful; but laughing at the same time and telling myself I'm darned right I'll be right back here on the next Friday night I'm in Lincoln for a game weekend. Even if I do have a dark secret I have neglected to tell these friendly folks.

The next morning, Terry Connealy and the Huskers, 5-0 and about to embark on their Big Eight Conference schedule against Oklahoma State, get their wakeup calls at 8 and are in chapel or mass by 8:30.

Now this is wholesome. I'm at the Big Red Breakfast on Saturday morning in the packed Ramada Inn meeting room. Former Cornhuskers play-by-play man Dick Perry holding court at the head table and broadcasting live on KMEM-AM, Lincoln's memories station.

Originally, it's my guess TSN photographer Doug DeVoe and I are the only ones in this room who were at the Sidetrack the night before. Then again, when I mention where we had been, enough of these folks laugh to make me wonder if they hadn't been out there singing along with Joyce, after all.

I'm invited up to the head table to talk with Dick Perry, on the microphone and on radio. I reveal that the genesis for this story was that I had suggested a look at a unique college football weekend, and that I knew I would find that in Lincoln. I say I knew this as far back as 1971, when my father, the head coach at Oregon, brought the Ducks into Lincoln for the opening game of what would be the Huskers' national championship season. On the morning of the game, Sellout No. 47, he picked up the phone in his Holiday Inn room on Cornhusker Highway. (Timeout: Half of everything in Lincoln is named Cornhusker something, I believe, and I can't understand why they haven't painted the Capitol dome, the tallest structure in town, red as well.) On the morning of that game, my father heard: "Good morning, Coach, it's 7 and this is your wake-up call. GO BIG RED!"

Then I tell the crowd that my first conversations with John Rawlings, the editor of TSN, went as follows:

Rawlings: "Terry, we usually only hire writers who have legitimate college degrees."

Me: "What do you mean? I've got a degree."

Rawlings, disdainfully: "I said 'legitimate.' You went to the University of Colorado."

There. These nice folks at the Big Red Breakfast not only laugh, but my secret is out. At least according to the alumni associations, I am a hated Colorado Buffalo.

Perry, a true gentleman, says I seem like a nice guy, but asks what TSN has against the Huskers, because even from our magazine, they don't seem to get enough . . . well, you can guess the rest. And his broadcasting partner, Bill Wood, asks on the air if I can't put in my vote to run all the boxscores again.

At the Nebraska Center, the Huskers go into group meetings at 9:30.

In front of the Sigma Nu fraternity, student Denny Franks first runs pass patterns across 16th Street, amidst traffic, then turns his attention to trying to coax drivers into turning into his fraternity's driveway. Franks, 19, jumps in the path of cars, waves, begs, screeches. He'll risk sacrificing his body to make drivers swerve or laugh—or both. The Nebraska fight song is blaring from a boom box.

It's three hours to game time.

"We have to try to get cars to park in our lot and get money," says Franks, from Omaha. "We can't let 'em by. We gotta stop 'em."

Football parking, five bucks a pop, with the money going to Sigma Nu's pledge function.

Franks and Ryan Anderson, 20, also of Omaha, are the chief parking recruiters while some of their fraternity brothers play catch in the front yard. Jason Rohrs of Syracuse, Neb., is sitting on a second-floor ledge, outside a window, shirtless and wearing a huge red-foam cowboy hat. Greg Metschke also is barechested, but he's wearing a red cape. I don't tug on it, and there isn't any wind to spit into. Metschke also is adept at recruiting parking customers, but has backed off a little since the time he "stiff-armed a bus."

I wonder: How did last night go, guys?

"It was the normal Friday night, staying up all night and getting ready for the Saturday morning of a game," Franks says. "We don't sleep Friday nights, otherwise we wouldn't be this wound up."

Franks pauses to holler at cars.

"Some of the people pass out," he says, "but we try and make people stay up all night, by keeping 'em up, making 'em go crazy, running around, blasting the stereos screaming."

Have I pointed out that fraternities at Nebraska officially are "dry"?

"That's why we have cups," says Metschke, who is holding a paper cup.

This is all a dry run—sorry, couldn't resist—for that game against the *hated* Colorado Buffaloes. "I think Colorado's doing all right now," Franks says, "but as soon as they come here, we'll see if they can really play."

There was a time in the not-so-ancient past when Oklahoma was the No. 1 opponent, and Colorado—while a rival—didn't trigger such indignant reactions in Lincoln. The rivalry clearly would have picked up after the Buffaloes resurgence in the late 1980s, but this needs to be acknowledged: If anybody got this *started*, the fingers should be pointing toward Boulder. McCartney essentially anointed the Cornhuskers as the chief rival, and he asked Colorado fans not to sell their tickets to Nebraska games in Boulder to anyone who might wear red to Folsom Field. Yes, Nebraskans overreacted to that, and at times Husker fans deserve the No. 1

ranking in a poll about paranoia. McCartney never suggested that Nebraska should be nuked, or that residents were sub-human slime. Arguably, he was paying a compliment to the depth of Nebraska loyalty and the Huskers' winning tradition. But I'll concede this: The Denver media—of which I also am an alum—often have portrayed Nebraska fans as, at best, hayseeds; and, at worst, straight from the banjo scene in "Deliverance." Finally, many of Colorado's fans at Folsom Field have treated Nebraska visitors with rudeness that goes beyond the usual Saturday stadium jeering of folks in the "wrong" colors. In the past, I've been at games in Lincoln at which badly beaten opponents get polite hands from the Nebraska fans as they come off the field, and until the rivalry heated up, it was hard to imagine Colorado fans being treated rudely in Lincoln.

So when I ask the Sigma Nu boys about why they don't like Colorado, the answer doesn't surprise me. "Because they suck," says Metschke, the man with the cape. "They decided they didn't like us, so we don't like them. Hey, what's his name—McCartney?—wanted to make it into a rivalry, so we'll take it to the end. He picked us as his rival, so they could rise to our level. But they can't."

The sound of tape tearing and the smell of fresh adhesive are football constants; nobody has figured out a "new" way to tape or otherwise protect ankles. At the Nebraska Center, the Huskers take turns having their ankles taped, then pull their socks back on. They won't be leaving for the nearby stadium for a few more minutes.

Despite the predictable game-week rhetoric from the Cornhuskers, nobody expects this Oklahoma State game to be much more than a walk-through, a warm-up for the bigger games later on. The ones in which the Huskers will find out whether their abundance of talent can overcome the loss of a superlative quarterback, Frazier. This remains a highly praiseworthy team, with a tremendous offensive line led by potential All-America tackle Zach Wiegert, a 6-5, 300-pounder from Fremont, Neb.; with an electric sophomore I-back, Lawrence Phillips; with a solid defensive front and linebacking corps that prevents a lack of defensive backfield depth from being a critical deficiency. At least so far. And with option-oriented Oklahoma State ranking 94th in the country in passing yardage going into the appearance in Lincoln, and with the Cowboys coming off a two-point victory over a bye called North Texas, there's no guarantee this won't be another romp for the Huskers.

Rich Stanwiak, who works in mail advertising in Omaha, is standing outside the stadium, decked out in a red Nebraska hat, a white Nebraska sweatshirt, red Nebraska sweatpants, and red-and-white shoes. He has been holding two fingers aloft for about 45 minutes and has turned down the scalpers who want $50 for $22 tickets. Finally, he closes a deal: $25 apiece.

He'll have to pay more for Colorado.

The 34-foot Pace Arrow is parked at the base of the foot bridge adjacent to the stadium. Blue Iowa plates are the most common evidence of out-of-state support for the Huskers in this season-pass lot, but the Pace Arrow is from South Dakota. The owners, Donna Vader and her husband, David, who has retired after a career in marine construction, live in Pickstown, S.D. "I'm D. Vader, like Darth," Donna says, "and I am spacey most of the time." The Vaders once lived in Omaha and have been going to Huskers games since the '70s.

The Vaders left home Friday morning. They stopped in David City, Neb., on Friday night, hooking up to Pat Comte's garage—"so we could have electricity and keep the beer cold," Donna says—and then visited Pat's establishment, the Comte Bar. Pat was aboard Saturday morning when the Pace Arrow left again at 6:30, and the final stop was in Osceola, to pick up Donald and Doris Ostberg, who had the coveted pass for the prime lot. "That's what friends are for, to use each other," Donna says. "We have the mobile home, and they have the parking spot. We hate each other, but we get along for the Nebraska games."

For the record, Doris Ostberg is aghast when that quote is read to her—and Donna Vader *is* kidding. In a few minutes, Muffy, the tiny dog with red ribbons around each ear, will be shut into the mobile home and the trailer contingent will enter the stadium to see if the Huskers can stay unbeaten against one of the worst teams in the Big Eight.

Section 30, Row 42, Seat 3 is above at the north goal line. Isabelle Lampshire, 91, of Lincoln, has been sitting here since the second year of the sellout streak, or since she and her husband, Wesley, obtained the season tickets in 1963.

"I've missed only two or three games," Isabelle says. "I don't remember which ones, except I know one was against Washington State and we lost."

That was Sellout No. 86, September 10, 1977.

"When I came back the next game," she says, "my buddies all around me blamed me for the loss because I had been gone."

That "next game," by the way, was the Alabama game—the one at which "little" Terry Connealy's name came booming over the public-address system. Isabelle doesn't remember that, but she has forgotten very little about the Huskers and her game-day experiences, both at Memorial Stadium and at the Devaney Center, where she has attended all but a handful of the men's basketball games since the building opened in 1976.

Isabelle goes to the games now with friends, or with her son, retired dentist Earl Lampshire; or her daughter, Virginia Hagerman. Wesley, Isabelle's husband, was a contractor. In November 1969, he was in considerable pain with leukemia but was determined to attend the last home game of the season, against Iowa State on November 8. "They gave him a transfusion," Earl says, "just so he'd be able to walk up to his seat. Devaney got him a special parking permit for under the stadium and he went to the game."

Wesley died November 20.

Twenty-five years later, Isabelle still has fun at these games. She's so good-natured, I was guessing she might say something good about the *hated* Buffaloes.

"I don't like Colorado," she says. Oh. "I've been to all the stadiums in the league except the Kansas ones. I was at Colorado one of the times, enjoying a good game, but three seats in front of me, I saw a Colorado fan pour a can of beer over some Nebraska people, and I thought that was terrible. Another time, we were going along the street and Earl had one of those nice red hats on. We had the window down and a guy reached in and stole his hat. So I didn't like Colorado."

Probably never will.

The Oklahoma State game is the Huskers' fourth at home in as many weeks. After beating UCLA—when that still was considered a significant accomplishment—Nebraska beat Pacific, 70-21, and then Wyoming, 42-32. The surprisingly tough victory over Wyoming was more alarming than encouraging. Although Berringer played well, he came out of the game with a partially collapsed lung.

Against Oklahoma State, Connealy gets a sack on the first defensive series and gets up pumping his arms in emotion. The Hyannis contingent goes nuts.

Thanks to turnovers and mistakes, the Cornhuskers lead only 9-3 at the half. At the break, Berringer rides in a squad car to the health center for a prescheduled test, and he knows the result will be trouble. The lung has partially deflated again, and he's held out of the second half. He watches from the sideline as Turman, the walk-on, plays a mistake-free game and the Huskers get three second half TDs. Phillips, one of the Californians, ends up running for 221 yards and three touchdowns, and the defense is dominant. This score might end up looking good enough for the poll voters, I'm thinking, but this is not the No. 2 team in the country after the loss of Frazier. The final—32-3—seems misleading. Besides, this was Oklahoma State, Turman wasn't asked to do too much—and the tough part of the schedule is about to begin.

For the moment, the fans are having fun with this latest saga of a walk-on hero. Turman now is the "Terminator" and he's treated as if he were Rocky Balboa after fighting Apollo Creed for the first time. Turman, poised and glib with the media, says quarterbacks coach Turner Gill—himself a former Nebraska quarterback—"told me to get in there, call the play, line up and take a deep breath and pretend like it was just another scrimmage. Then, when I saw the offensive line just blowing people off the ball and the defense play an incredible game, I felt pretty comfortable."

Fans and families are waiting outside the main door to the athletic complex at the south side of the stadium. Players greet their families or sign autographs, or both. Undetected, Berringer leaves from a side door, walking slowly.

After showering, dressing and briefly meeting with the media, Terry Connealy heads straight to the Ramada, where the meeting room—the same one used for the Big Red Breakfast—is jammed. Every man, woman and child from Hyannis seems to be there, and every one of them seems to have brought another man, woman or child. Maybe half of them are wearing the T-shirts. This is a town meeting, 320 miles from town.

When he arrives, Terry makes it about 11 feet into the room in the first 15 minutes, looking like a U.S. Senate candidate about to go to the podium and claim victory—but he has to wade through the crowd first.

"I hope we don't have any prairie fires," Marty Connealy says. "We won't have anybody there to put them out."

Finally, Nebraska defensive coordinator Charlie McBride—an 18-year veteran of the Huskers staff—grabs the microphone, calls the Connealy clan up next to him and gives a heartfelt tribute to Terry as one of McBride's career favorites. "And I've got to say that in all my years here," McBride says, smiling, "this is the biggest mess I've ever seen."

The next home game, Sellout No. 200, is against Coach Bill McCartney and the *hated* Colorado Buffaloes. The good folks of Hyannis, and much of the nation, will be watching on television. And not all of them will know what they're missing by not being a part of game weekend in Lincoln.

NEBRASKA'S DEFENSE DELIVERS

From The Associated Press

MANHATTAN, Kan., Oct. 15, 1994—A strong defensive performance and the running of Lawrence Phillips helped No. 2-ranked Nebraska defeat No. 16 Kansas State, 17-6, in a Big Eight showdown on a dreary, rainy Saturday.

Kansas State quarterback Chad May, a transfer from Cal State Fullerton, threw a 29-yard touchdown pass to Mitch Running early in the second quarter, but rain that started falling after halftime took away his 249 yards on a 22-of-48 day.

"Some of them slipped out of my hands," said May, who had passed for a Big Eight-record 489 yards against Nebraska last year. "But I can't make excuses. They had a very good pass rush. It's kind of hard to throw with guys in your face."

Nebraska clung to a 7-6 lead until a 15-yard run by Jeff Makovicka with about 11 minutes to play broke the game open. The Cornhuskers won their 21st consecutive regular-season game and beat Kansas State for the 26th consecutive time.

"Our secondary really played outstanding because they have got a great quarterback," Nebraska defensive coordinator Charlie McBride said. "If you would have told me we'd hold them to six points, I wouldn't have believed you.

"I heard some guy in the hotel say last night that we were OK, but that our only problem was the secondary. Well, today it wasn't."

Phillips ran for 126 yards in 31 carries for his seventh consecutive 100-yard game and scored the first touchdown of the game. The Nebraska defense made it stand up until Makovicka burst through a big hole in the fourth quarter.

"It's my first touchdown of the season. I guess it was a good place to get it," Makovicka said. "We came into their lair and they played well against us. But it was the offensive line who opened the hole. I just happened to have the ball.

"They are called the pipeline. We have the best offensive line in the nation. There's a feeling at Nebraska that if we stay in the game until the fourth quarter, we're going to win. I had that feeling on the sidelines today."

Sophomore walk-on quarterback Matt Turman started the game and played most of the first half, spending his time handing off to Phillips. The Huskers (7-0, 2-0) had only 18 passing yards by the end of the third quarter.

Brook Berringer played the final series of the first half and the second half as the Huskers try to replace Tommie Frazier, out for the season with blood clots in his leg.

The Huskers blocked Martin Gramatica's extra-point try after holder Matt Miller fumbled the snap following the only touchdown by the Wildcats (4-1, 1-1).

"We had problems with penalties and that put us in a hole," Kansas State Coach Bill Snyder said. "We also had difficulty running the ball. Our field position in the second half was terrible.

"All losses are painful. I just told our players that the more investment you put in the game, the greater the loss."

The Wildcats using four and five wide receivers throughout, outgained the Huskers most of the game, but mistakes and poor field position conspired to keep them out of the end zone after the lone score and they remained winless at home against Nebraska since 1959.

NEBRASKA VS. KANSAS STATE

Jeff Makovicka scored his first touchdown of the year on a 15-yard run in the fourth quarter.

KANSAS STATE GETS A DOSE OF HUSKER REALITY

By WILLIAM C. RHODEN
New York Times

MANHATTAN, Kan., Oct. 15, 1994—After a week of sunny skies and cheerful optimism, Kansas State was pummeled into a deep purple funk this afternoon by Nebraska. The Cornhuskers, who started a walk-on at quarterback and temporarily lost their leading rusher, overcame the losses with a crushing defensive performance and earned a 17-6 victory at K.S.U. Stadium.

With a chilling day-long rain falling, the Wildcats' high-flying offense, led by quarterback Chad May, was shut down by a Nebraska defense that blitzed, harried and manhandled May into having one of the poorest days of his career.

Last year, May threw for a Big Eight-record 489 yards against Nebraska. Today, May was sacked 6 times and completed only 22 of 48 attempts for 249 yards. He threw a touchdown pass, but was intercepted for the first time in more than 180 attempts going back to last season.

Nebraska (7-0 over all, 2-0 in the Big Eight) came into the game ranked No. 2 in both major national polls and No. 4 in The New York Times computer rankings. Kansas State was 16th-ranked in the Associated Press poll, 11th ranked in the USA TODAY/CNN poll and No. 1 in The Times's ranking.

The Huskers got their 26th consecutive victory over Kansas State (4-1, 1-1).

Nebraska clung to the one-point lead until an 11-play, 75-yard drive finished off the Wildcats. Jeff Makovicka's 15-yard scoring run with 11:01 to play widened the margin and Darin Erstad kicked a 24-yard field goal with 1:32 remaining.

Lawrence Phillips, who rushed 31 times for 126 yards and a touchdown, gets assistance from tackle Rob Zatechka.

"The weather was ugly and cold — it was just a Nebraska kind of day," said Charlie McBride, the Cornhusker defensive coordinator.

"If you had told me we'd hold Kansas State to 6 points, I wouldn't have believed you. But I thought our secondary played unbelievable. There were a couple quotes that put some life in our players. One was that if we played man to man they were going to get some big plays. The other was that they knew where our seams were and would pick us apart. That gave us an emotional lift."

The greatest lift was provided by Lawrence Phillips, the 6-foot, 200-pound sophomore running back, who scored one touchdown and battered Kansas State for 126 yards on 31 carries. Phillips was forced out of the game near the end of the first half when he hurt his left hand after being hit on an incomplete pass. He didn't return until a little more than six minutes remained in the third quarter.

Nebraska gained 226 yards on the ground while Kansas State was minus 62 yards.

This was an especially crushing loss for a surging team looking to beat Nebraska at home for the first time since 1959. If the Wildcats were going to do it, this would be the year. They had a veteran team and the nation's hottest quarterback. More than that, Nebraska was playing its third game without Tommie Frazier, the junior quarterback who was a one-time Heisman Trophy candidate. Frazier is out for the season with blood clots in his right leg. Matt Turman, a sophomore non-scholarship player, started the game.

Nebraska 17
Kansas St. 6

Nebraska	7	0	0	10	– 17
Kansas St.	0	6	0	0	– 6

NU—Phillips 2 run (Erstad kick)
KSU—Running 29 pass from May (kick blocked)
NU—Makovicka 15 run (Erstad kick)
NU—Erstad FG 24
A—42,817

TEAM STATISTICS

Category	Neb	KSt.
First downs	16	17
Rushes-yards	50-168	23-(-7)
Passing yards	52	249
Return yards	74	17
Passes	4-11-0	22-48-1
Punts	7-37	8-36
Fumbles-lost	2-1	2-0
Penalties-yards	9-70	12-102
Time of possession	31:26	28:34

INDIVIDUAL STATISTICS
RUSHING: Nebraska—Phillips 31-126, Makovicka 7-5, Schlesinger 3-24, Turman 4-10, Berringer 2-5, Childs 2-0, Benning 1-(minus 2). Kansas St.—J. Smith 14-29, May 9-(minus 36).
PASSING: Nebraska—Berringer 2-7-0-37, Turman 2-4-0-15, Kansas St.—May 22-48-1-249.
RECEIVING: Nebraska—Muhammad 1-34, Phillips 2-15, Childs 1-3. Kansas St.—Running 5-79, Lockett 5-78, R. Brown 3-44, J. Smith 6-29, Schwieger 3-19.

ASSOCIATED PRESS TOP 10

	Team	Rec.	Votes	LW
1.	Penn State (19)	6-0-0	1,487	3
2.	Colorado (15)	6-0-0	1,474	4
3.	Nebraska (25)	7-0-0	1,463	2
4.	Auburn (3)	7-0-0	1,402	6
5.	Florida	5-1-0	1,196	1
6.	Texas A&M	6-0-0	1,188	7
7.	Miami (Fla.)	4-1-0	1,131	8
8.	Alabama	7-0-0	1,130	10
9.	Washington	5-1-0	1,128	9
10.	Florida State	4-1-0	1,021	11

USA TODAY/CNN TOP 10

	Team	Rec.	Votes	LW
1.	Penn State (22)	6-0-0	1,504	3
2.	Nebraska (31)	7-0-0	1,498	2
3.	Colorado (9)	6-0-0	1,458	4
4.	Miami (Fla.)	4-1-0	1,283	7
5.	Alabama	7-0-0	1,271	6
6.	Florida	5-1-0	1,254	1
7.	Florida State	4-1-0	1,188	8
8.	Arizona	5-1-0	997	10
9.	Texas	4-2-0	975	9
10.	North Carolina	5-1-0	935	12

NEBRASKA AVOIDS NEW DISASTERS

From The Associated Press

Two of Damon Benning's 10 rushes resulted in touchdowns.

COLUMBIA, Mo., Oct. 23, 1994—Nebraska Coach Tom Osborne only wanted his quarterback to avoid injury. Brook Berringer gave him much more.

Berringer, back as the starter after missing half of last week's game with a partially collapsed lung, threw three touchdown passes in the second half as the third-ranked Cornhuskers (8-0, 3-0) overcame a slow start to beat Missouri, 42-7, Saturday.

"Brook can do it all," Osborne said. "Next week, he'll have to do it all."

Nebraska, which also got 110 yards rushing from Lawrence Phillips, is at home against No. 2 Colorado next weekend.

"I wanted to try to get Berringer through today without getting hit, and I don't think he took any bad blows," Osborne said. "Obviously, we can't sit on anything now."

Berringer sat out the first half of last week's 17-6 victory over Kansas State with a partially collapsed lung. He wore a flak jacket in that game, and against Missouri, Osborne cut back on his use of the option attack to protect Berringer for the bigger games ahead.

"We run the option well, but we've got other options," said Berringer, who completed nine of 13 passes for 153 yards. "We can throw the ball, we can hand it off, we can do a lot of things."

Nebraska didn't have a first down in a scoreless first quarter, yet the issue was never in doubt. Missouri, which has lost five in a row at home, averted a shutout on a 34-yard touchdown pass from Jeff Handy to Rahsetnu Jenkins with 7:34 to play.

After the game, Missouri Coach Larry Smith could be heard screaming at his players behind closed doors to "hold yourselves accountable." He said the team gave up after falling behind, 28-0.

"It wasn't a pretty sight," Smith said. "It wasn't a pretty sight at all. I'm angry, I'm disappointed and

NEBRASKA VS. MISSOURI

▲ **Defensive back Barron Miles forced a fumble in the end zone to kill a Missouri scoring drive and later returned an interception 27 yards to set up a Nebraska score.**

NEBRASKA VS. MISSOURI

they'd better be angry and disappointed too because those last three touchdowns never needed to be scored."

Nebraska has allowed 16 points in its last three games. Defensive back Barron Miles ended a Missouri scoring chance when he forced Joe Freeman to fumble into the end zone from the one and returned an interception 27 yards to set up a Nebraska score.

The Cornhuskers also have won 21 in a row in the regular season, 12 in a row in the Big Eight, and have a 16-game winning streak against Missouri (2-5 1-2). The last six meetings have been by a cumulative 307-72 score.

Phillips recorded his eighth consecutive 100-yard game and scored on a five-yard run for the game's first touchdown.

Nebraska 42
Missouri 7

Nebraska	0	14	14	14	— 42
Missouri	0	0	0	7	— 7

Neb—Phillips 5 run (Sieler kick)
Neb—Benning 9 run (Sieler kick)
Neb—Gilman 1 pass from Berringer (Erstad kick)
Neb—Holbein 30 pass from Berringer (Erstad kick)
Mis—Jenkins 34 pass from Handy (Pooler kick)
Neb—Baul 43 pass from Berringer (Erstad kick)
Neb—Benning 2 run (Erstad kick)
Attendance—50,537

TEAM STATISTICS

Category	Neb	Mis
First downs	23	13
Rushes-yards	58-334	29-48
Net. yd. passing	152	150
Return yards	97	53
Passes	9-13-0	19-32-1
Punts	4-42	9-40
Fumbles-lost	2-1	3-1
Penalties-yards	9-75	5-50
Time of possession	31:31	28:29

INDIVIDUAL STATISTICS
RUSHING: Nebraska—Phillips 22-110; Childs 6-65; Benning 10-43; Schlesinger 5-35; Berringer 5-23; Turman 1-21; Makovicka 5-18; Schuster 3-14; Muhammad 1-5. Missouri—Olivo 11-37; Freeman 11-26; Janes 2-10; Washington 1-0; Handy 4-(-25).
PASSING: Nebraska—Berringer 9-13-0, 152. Missouri—Handy 19-29-1, 150; Corso 0-3-0, 0.
RECEIVING: Nebraska—Benning 2-20; Muhammad 2-23; Gilman 2-7; Baul 1-43; Holbein 1-30; Alford 1-29. Missouri—Jenkins 8-90; Sallee 5-38; S. Jones 2-15; Frazier 2-5; Olivo 1-1; Janes 1-1.

ASSOCIATED PRESS TOP 10

	Team	Rec.	Votes	LW
1.	Penn St. (19)	6-0-0	1,486	1
2.	Colorado (16)	7-0-0	1,482	2
3.	Nebraska (24)	8-0-0	1,461	3
4.	Auburn (3)	7-0-0	1,397	4
5.	Florida	5-1-0	1,246	5
6.	Miami (Fla.)	5-1-0	1,187	7
7.	Texas A&M	7-0-0	1,171	6
8.	Alabama	8-0-0	1,165	8
9.	Florida St.	5-1-0	1,076	10
10.	Michigan	5-2-0	998	11

USA TODAY/CNN TOP 10

	Team	Rec.	Votes	LW
1.	Penn St. (28)	6-0-0	1,507	1
2.	Nebraska (25)	8-0-0	1,492	2
3.	Colorado (9)	7-0-0	1,459	3
4.	Miami (Fla.)	5-1-0	1,318	4
5.	Alabama	8-0-0	1,300	5
6.	Florida	5-1-0	1,245	6
7.	Florida St.	5-1-0	1,166	7
8.	Arizona	6-1-0	1,093	8
9.	Michigan	5-2-0	979	12
10.	Virginia Tech	7-1-0	928	13

Brendan Holbein snared a 30-yard pass from Berringer to assemble 28 unanswered points against Missouri.

Nebraska-Colorado Stakes High

By STEVE WIEBERG
USA TODAY

Harvard-Yale, maybe it ain't.

But what used to be an annual, and forgettable, tuneup for Big Eight power Nebraska—against Colorado—is escalating into a top rivalry in college football.

The unbeaten teams meet Saturday in Lincoln, Neb., with the stakes now typically high. They're ranked 2-3 in the polls, the fourth time in six years each has been in the top 10. The last five winners have gone on to a Big Eight championship and the Orange Bowl. A 1991 tie sent Nebraska to Miami.

To Nebraska coach Tom Osborne, it's a matter of circumstance: "When both programs are playing well, it's obviously a big game. And it's that way this week."

To Colorado's Bill McCartney, the ex-Michigan assistant who wanted an equivalent to the Wolverines' rivalry with Ohio State, it's by design: "It seemed like the logical team, the bordering state, would be Nebraska. They were a lot better than us then, but we still went through with it.

"They've made it pretty obvious they don't consider us a rival," he says. "But we'll always make them the red-letter game on our schedule."

LAWRENCE PHILLIPS

PHILLIPS FILLS OFFENSIVE GAP WITH BIG RUNS

By STEVE WIEBERG
USA TODAY

LINCOLN, Neb., Oct. 26, 1994—No Tommie Frazier. No option game to speak of. No mystery.

Opposing defenses have massed the past couple weeks to stop what they knew was coming—what had to come—from Nebraska's gutted offense. Lawrence Phillips right. Phillips left. Phillips up the middle.

"It's a time when you know you're going to have to pound it out and get whatever you can," Phillips says, "and maybe once or twice, you might get a 20- or 25-yarder."

What the sophomore tailback got against those bunched-up, zeroed-in, eight-man lines was 117 yards and a TD rushing at Kansas State, 110 yards and a TD at Missouri. More important, what the Cornhuskers (8-0) got was a couple of wins to preserve their No. 2 ranking in the USA TODAY/CNN Coaches poll and a shot at a national championship. They take both into Saturday's showdown against Colorado.

A couple other backs have run for as many or more yards as Phillips, who's averaging 154 a game this season. Several have more fame and support among Heisman Trophy voters.

None, however, has worked any harder, even though Phillips is running behind perhaps the best offensive line in the nation.

Frazier was lost to recurring blood clots in his leg, and backup Brook Berringer was out for awhile with a partially collapsed lung. Nebraska completed just four passes at Kansas State, nine at Missouri, and all but eliminated its option running game. Phillips might as well have worn a bulls-eye.

"Brook is healthy now, and we can get the rest of our offense in," says Phillips. "I don't think it'll be focused on me as much as it was the last few weeks. It'll take some of the pressure off."

Of his 12 touchdowns this season, Phillips has scored eight in the four games without Frazier. His 1,233 yards are 320 shy of the Big Eight record for a sophomore, set in 1985 by Oklahoma State's Thurman Thomas.

"The biggest thing," Berringer says, "is he's played with a lot of heart."

The team was afraid Phillips had broken his left thumb when he banged it against a helmet at Kansas State. X-rays taken at halftime showed it was severely sprained but unbroken, and he returned midway through the third quarter to rush for 64 of his 117 yards.

Still bothered by the injury, he essentially played one-armed at Missouri.

"Of all the tailbacks I've ever seen here," linebacker Ed Stewart says, "he's as good or better." Which is significant, given that Stewart has played in previous years' practices against Derek Brown and Calvin Jones, now with the NFL's New Orleans Saints and Los Angeles Rams, respectively.

"Historically, Nebraska tailbacks are real rugged runners," says Colorado coach Bill McCartney. "They run hard and they run tough . . .

"Phillips is out of that mold. And he only figures to get better and better."

Kansas State targeted its defense on Lawrence Phillips, but he still ran for 117 yards and a TD.

QB BERRINGER BEARS BURDEN FOR HUSKERS

By STEVE WIEBERG
USA TODAY

Berringer proved that he had recovered from his injuries by completing 9 of 13 passes for 153 yards, and throwing three touchdown passes in the second half to beat Missouri 42-7.

LINCOLN, Neb., Oct. 28, 1994—A "minor setback," Brook Berringer calls it.

Tommie Frazier is lost for the rest of Nebraska's season. The Cornhuskers scratch not only a Heisman Trophy-contending quarterback but the most important component in a national championship-contending team. He was their heart, if not also their soul.

Minor?

That's the way Frazier's replacement sees it. He might be alone. "There've been a lot of people who haven't given me a chance," Berringer says. "I don't know what it'll take. I suppose winning a national championship is the only way."

The opportunity awaits. The No. 2-ranked Huskers have survived four games without Frazier, to arrive Saturday at a pivotal fifth: vs. No. 3 Colorado (noon ET, ABC).

The ramifications are long-range. The winner will challenge now-No. 1 Penn State—if the Nittany Lions beat Ohio State at home; they're favored by two touchdowns—for the top spot in Sunday's new polls. And there, at No. 1 or No. 2, they're very likely to stay the rest of the regular season, given their remaining schedules.

With a playoff, no matter. But without one, and with No. 2 denied a shot at No. 1 in a bowl, it matters. A lot.

The Nebraska-Colorado winner, as likely Big Eight champion, will head to the Orange Bowl. Penn State, as the likely Big Ten champ, will pack for Pasadena, Calif., and the Rose.

Consider Nebraska and Colorado are 2-3 in both polls and account for 34 of 62 first-place votes in the USA TODAY/CNN coaches' rankings and 40 of 62 in The Associated Press media poll. Consider the possibility the winner will inherit the bulk of the loser's electoral support and leapfrog Penn State. And the importance of Saturday's showdown in the Huskers' Memorial Stadium is clear.

Just as clear: the heavy responsibility borne by Berringer, a junior with 17 college completions before this fall.

He has emerged from a series of misfortunes that fate, for whatever reason, piled on the Huskers. "It has been a little more of a chess game, I guess, than we've normally had," coach Tom Osborne says. "But I don't think it's been insurmountable."

Frazier's season was ended by recurring blood

clots in his leg. Then Berringer was felled, twice, by a partially collapsed lung, and Nebraska inserted walk-on Matt Turman. Now Turman is nursing a bruised shoulder, and another walk-on, the exquisitely named Monte Christo, is on alert.

The secondary has been thinned, as well, by a season-ending knee injury to safety Mike Minter.

As lineman Rob Zatechka says, the Huskers have "done a good job of rolling with the punches." They've leaned on running back Lawrence Phillips, that 295-pounds-a-man offensive line and the nation's best running game. Their defense, infused in recent years with quickness and speed, has stepped up, allowing an average of 29 yards rushing in their last four games and a total of 16 points in their last three.

And they've continued to win. Not with pop. Not with sizzle. Berringer returned, but to protect his tender upper body, Nebraska fitted him with a Robocop-esque flak jacket and abandoned its option game. The offense against Kansas State and Missouri the last two weeks has been a succession of straight handoffs and dives and few safe passes—keeping the quarterback as far out of harm's way as possible. Deadly dull, but deadly effective.

Berringer is no Frazier. But he's a 60% passer, and coming off a career-best 152-yard, three-TD performance at Missouri. With enough attempts, he'd be among the nation's top 25 in efficiency.

"I don't want to say he's a better passer than Tommie, but he's a good passer," Colorado coach Bill McCartney says. "Berringer's more of a prototype thrower. He's rangy; he's 6-4. He sets up well."

Berringer couldn't help but hear all the naysaying when Frazier was sidelined, and took offense. "I came into a tough situation where a lot of people maybe had some question whether I'd be able to get it done," he says. "To most people who know anything about football, I think we've proved we can still move the football, that we're still Nebraska and we're going to get it done."

His lung is now "100 percent," he says. And Osborne is preparing to let him off his short leash, to reinstate the Frazier-less option attack against Colorado.

That's as much by necessity as choice. The Buffaloes are hardly Missouri or even Kansas State. They're No. 2 in the nation in total offense and averaging better than 40 points a game. They have the Heisman front-runner in tailback Rashaan Salaam and a second candidate in quarterback Kordell Stewart. They've beaten five ranked teams, including Michigan on the season's most memorable play.

Oddsmakers rate the game even. Accounting for the usual three-point concession for home-field advantage, that means they like Colorado, which has lost only five of its last 35 on the road and two of its last seven against top-five opponents.

Two years ago, however, the Buffaloes came to Lincoln and were embarrassed 52-7. Last season, Stewart threw three interceptions and was sacked four times, and they lost 21-17 in Boulder, Colo.

Those are the only black marks on Colorado's 33-2-3 record in the Big Eight since '88.

And as Nebraska's Phillips notes, "We've kind of got our backs to the wall." Just as the Huskers did in last season's Orange Bowl, where they were unrespected 17-point underdogs but didn't fall to Florida State until a last-play missed field goal.

"One minor setback (the loss of Frazier), and it's all back," Berringer says. "'You can't do this. You can't do that.' . . . We lose our respect."

The antidote: a win Saturday, en route to a national championship. "That's what we can do," Berringer says, "and I think that's what we're going to do."

NEBRASKA CAN'T BLOCK IMAGE

By J.A. ADANDE
Washington Post

LINCOLN, Neb., Oct. 27, 1994—The kind of season Nebraska has had only makes sense if you've been here a while. You get used to certain aspects of life around these parts. The winning season and sellout crowds at Memorial Stadium are constants. So is the search for respect.

As it stands, the Cornhuskers had more respect after losing to Florida State in the Orange Bowl on Jan. 1 than they do now, even though they've won every game since.

"We went through an undefeated season [in 1993] and still didn't get a lot of respect until after the bowl game, which we lost, which doesn't make much sense," defensive tackle Terry Connealy said. "But I think everybody's used to being in that situation here at Nebraska."

A quick look at the illogical process that has been their 1994 season: They keep winning despite losing quarterbacks to injury almost weekly; they lost the No. 1 ranking without losing a game; when Auburn upset Florida on Oct. 8, throwing the top spot in the Associated Press poll up for grabs, Nebraska went *down* a spot, to No. 3, despite beating then-No. 16 Kansas State on the road.

"You get tired of people putting you down, saying you're going to lose every week, you can't win games because you lost one person, your style of football's outdated and all this," tackle Zach Weigert said. "You keep winning games and still you don't get any respect. It gets old."

There's one way to change that.

"You earn respect," Weigert said. "I'm sure if we win our big games then we'll gain respect."

That's why when Nebraska (8-0, 3-0 Big Eight) faces No. 2 Colorado (7-0, 3-0) Saturday before the 200th consecutive sellout crowd at Memorial Stadium, it will be about more than titles. It will be about image and perceptions.

The Huskers belong in an elite group by most measures of college football excellence. The Nebraska media guide touts 32 consecutive winning seasons, 25 consecutive nine-victory seasons, 25 consecutive bowl bids (including 13 consecutive New Year's Day appearances), all National Collegiate Athletic Association records. So why is this the only state that thinks of the Huskers as winners?

"I guess everyone looks on the downside when they think about us," Wiegert said. "Maybe it's because we haven't won a bowl game in seven years."

Bingo. Under Coach Tom Osborne, who is in his 22nd season, Nebraska has a 214-47-3 overall record, but an 8-13 bowl record and zero national championships. The Huskers were the lower-ranked team in each of their last seven bowl games. The bottom line is that the Huskers can beat all of the Big Eight opponents they want, but they won't be acknowledged nationally until they win a big bowl game. Every trip to the Orange Bowl winds up as more ammunition for naysayers who claim that a soft schedule doesn't prepare a team for real competition, that running the ball between the tackles (as the Huskers did in 40 of 61 plays in one game this season) is no way to win a championship.

It's the burden of being a Nebraska fan. Dane Nannen, 27, grew up in Lincoln but spent the past three years in New York before returning this summer. "Nebraska has the reputation of having success in the regular season but being a choker when the games count," he learned during his time outside the state. "I don't think they get the respect they deserve."

And when they get it, it doesn't last long. On Jan. 1, the Cornhuskers lost the Orange Bowl and national championship to Florida State, 18-16, when Byron Bennett's 45-yard field goal attempt went wide left on the last play. The Huskers, 17 1/2-point underdogs, had outplayed the Seminoles and were on the bad end of a couple of questionable calls by the officials, but they definitely had a better offseason than Florida State. While the Seminoles were rocked by allegations of agent-funded player shopping sprees, the Cornhuskers basked in their newfound respect.

"I was kind of surprised that [the response] was as positive as it was," Osborne said. "I guess the perception was that we didn't have much of a chance. We didn't feel that way, but I think a lot of people did. When we played well enough to win or at least have a good shot at it, some people responded as if it were a win."

That carried into the first game of the season, when Nebraska rolled over defending Big East champion West Virginia, 31-0. Quarterback Tommie Frazier jumped into contention for the Heisman Trophy. The Huskers replaced preseason No. 1 Florida at the top of the Associated Press poll and it looked as if they controlled their chances for that elusive national championship.

They quickly found out that sometimes winning every game is not enough. First they slipped to No. 2 when Florida's explosive offense put up impressive numbers and caused enough voters to push the Gators back on top. On Sept. 25 they learned Frazier has a blood clot behind his right knee, and when it reformed the next week he was lost for the season.

Frazier's backup, Brook Berringer, suffered a partially collapsed lung against Wyoming on Oct. 1, but finished the game. He had to come out at halftime against Oklahoma State after the lung collapsed again. Sophomore walk-on Matt Turman started against Kansas State and played at the end of the Missouri game last week, but suffered a bruised shoulder on a late hit with 2:34 remaining, leaving this week's backup duties to freshman Monte Christo.

"It was like somebody did wrong around here and God was trying to pay us back for it," linebacker Ed Stewart said of the quarterback injuries.

Yet the Huskers kept winning, mostly thanks to I-back Lawrence Phillips, who has carried 184 times for 1,233 yards and 12 touchdowns.

"I think in many cases the perception has been that once Tommie Frazier got hurt, we were pretty well finished as a national championship contender," Osborne said. "I don't necessarily think that's true, but that's part of the perception that's out there. Sometimes perception is more powerful than reality."

According to tackle Zach Wiegert (72), there is only one way to make sure the Huskers are taken seriously: "You earn respect," he said. "I'm sure if we win our big games then we'll gain respect."

DEFENSE MUST DO THE JOB

By ANDREW BAGNATO
Chicago Tribune

LINCOLN, Neb., Oct. 29, 1994—Before Nebraska began changing quarterbacks faster than sweatsocks, the Cornhuskers defense needed only to be adequate. If the defense had a bad day, quarterback Tommie Frazier and tailback Lawrence Phillips would figure out a way to outscore the other side.

But with the offense in turmoil and a showdown with second-ranked Colorado (7-0) looming in Lincoln, the pressure has been placed squarely on the Big Red defense. That means the most important Cornhusker on the field Saturday might be linebacker Ed Stewart, a fifth-year senior out of Mt. Carmel High School.

"Being on the defensive side of the ball, you always think you have to win the game," said Stewart, one of 13 semifinalists for the Butkus Award, given to the nation's top linebacker.

To win this game, the third-ranked Cornhuskers (8-0) need to clamp down on the high-flying Buffaloes, who score from near and far and in the air and on the ground. The Buffaloes throw the nation's leading rusher, Rashaan Salaam (179.4 yards a game), and the No. 5 passer, Kordell Stewart (1,330 yards and seven touchdowns), at the opposition and watch the scoreboard explode.

The Buffaloes have defeated five ranked schools in the last six weeks—Wisconsin, Michigan, Texas, Oklahoma and Kansas State.

Colorado is averaging 40 points and 503 yards a game. If the Buffaloes put up anything close to those numbers Saturday, they will win by a rout.

"It's the best Colorado team I've played against," said Oklahoma coach Gary Gibbs, whose Sooners received a 45-7 drubbing from Colorado two weeks ago. "I have to give them the edge over those other [Buffalo powerhouses in 1989 and 1990]."

So it's up to Stewart and his crew. The Nebraska defense looked terrible in a scary 42-32 victory over mediocre Wyoming Oct. 1, but the unit has been nearly perfect since, allowing only 16 points in 12 quarters. Of course, two of its most recent outings came against Oklahoma State and Missouri, which would have trouble scoring against air.

Nebraska ranks third in the country against the rush, yielding 60 yards a game, and 12th in points allowed (13 per outing).

Cornhusker coaches give much of the credit to Stewart, who has seen his responsibilities increase since the Cornhuskers lost free safety Mike Minter, the secondary's "quarterback," for the season in the second game.

On Saturday, the Cornhuskers probably will turn Stewart loose for blitzes on Colorado quarterback Kordell Stewart. The Buffaloes had trouble picking up blitzes and stunts last week against Kansas State.

"Ed blitzes so hard that he peels the skin off his eyeballs," Cornhusker defensive coordinator Charlie McBride said. "That's how hard he plays all the time."

Blitzing requires Stewart to commit to a single point of attack. But when Kordell Stewart dances outside on the option, Ed Stewart can't commit until he has read the play.

"He can cover the pass like a defensive back, yet he's tough against the run," Nebraska coach Tom Osborne said. "We think he's a great player."

At 6 feet 1 inches and 215 pounds, Stewart is small for a linebacker. He was recruited as a strong safety but switched positions during his redshirt freshman year.

Stewart made the move reluctantly. He weighed only 190 pounds and thought he would be pounded by the Big Eight's massive linemen and fullbacks. But Stewart hit the weight room and bulked up without losing speed.

"You've got a kid with great mobility playing linebacker," Buffalo coach Bill McCartney said. "He's got the kind of maneuverability you expect in strong safeties. He's a tremendous football player. He plays with great spirit and intensity."

Stewart, who has earned a bachelor's degree in psychology, doesn't let his spirit bubble over off the field. Like many Cornhuskers, he has adopted Osborne's tight-lipped approach to the press. He won't be heard making brash predictions like another Butkus semifinalist, Dana Howard of Illinois.

Back in August, after the Cornhuskers disposed of West Virginia in the Kickoff Classic, Stewart allowed that Howard was the leading Butkus candidate.

"Hopefully, I can sneak up on him," said Stewart, his eyes twinkling.

With the offensive attack down, the pressure will be on the Husker defense in Saturday's game against Colorado. From left to right, Donta Jones, Ed Stewart and Phil Ellis.

HUSKERS SHRED BUFFALOES

By J.A. ADANDE
Washington Post

LINCOLN, Neb., Oct. 30, 1994—Rarely has the hyperbole of a souvenir sweat shirt been so appropriate.

"No fifth downs," read the anti-Colorado sweat shirt for sale in the Nebraska "Big Red" gift shop. "no Hail Marys. No chance."

Today, the Buffaloes didn't benefit from an official's oversight, as they did in their 1990 national championship season, and they didn't get a last-second, 64-yard pass, as they did in their dramatic victory Sept. 24 against Michigan. Instead, the No. 2 Buffaloes got a frustrating day in which No. 3 Nebraska thoroughly dominated the anticipated Big Eight showdown and won, 24-7, to offer its best argument as to why it should have the top spot in the polls.

"I hope the voters watched this game," Nebraska offensive tackle Zach Wiegert said. "We played a team that had played a tough schedule and beat them convincingly."

A crowd of 76,131, the school's 200th consecutive sellout at Memorial Stadium, saw Nebraska improve to 9-0 and all but lock up the Big Eight championship and the Orange Bowl bid that accompanies it with a 4-0 conference record. Colorado fell to 7-1, 3-1.

Husker linebacker Donta Jones celebrates sacking Colorado quarterback Kordell Stewart.

NEBRASKA VS. COLORADO

Brook Berringer is pressured by a Buffalo defender. Berringer completed 12 passes for 142 yards.

NEBRASKA VS. COLORADO

JOE MIXAN

> The Colorado match was the pivotal game of the Huskers' 1994 season. Coach Osborne views field action during Nebraska's big 24–7 win.

"This was the Orange Bowl game," Colorado linebacker Matt Russell said. "We're not going and they are."

In the fourth quarter, as if to further bury Colorado's championship hopes, the public address announcer kept updating the scores of what eventually would be losses by Michigan and Texas. The Buffaloes had staked much of their claim for a top ranking on beating those teams on the road in consecutive weeks, but the Wolverines' and Longhorns' recent slumps (two losses in the past three games for each team) are starting to lessen the magnitude of those victories.

And Colorado didn't show anything resembling championship form. The Buffaloes failed to convert any of their 11 third-down situations and were 0-for-4 on fourth down. They made bad passes and bad decisions. Nebraska players claimed Colorado players lost their will to win in the second half.

"We can speculate on any number of things," Colorado Coach Bill McCartney said, "but what we ought to speculate on is Nebraska outplayed us."

In a throwback type of game, the Cornhuskers won the battle of the front lines. Their offense ran basic plays and the line blew open huge holes that allowed the backs to gain 203 yards rushing. Their defensive line held the Buffaloes to 155 yards rushing, about half of Colorado's average.

Fullback Cory Schlesinger initiated Nebraska scoring with a 14-yard touchdown run in the first quarter. Nebraska totaled 203 rushing yards against a Colorado defense that had been yielding an average of only 99.7 yards a game.

NEBRASKA VS. COLORADO

I-back Clinton Childs (26) stares into the face of All-American Colorado cornerback Chris Hudson (47). Childs scored Nebraska's second touchdown to put the Huskers ahead 17-0 in the second quarter.

JOE MIXAN

Tight end Eric Alford pulled in a 30-yard Brook Berringer pass in the third quarter for the final Husker touchdown.

DENNIS HUBBARD

NEBRASKA VS. COLORADO

"I thought our defense was tremendous," Nebraska Coach Tom Osborne said. "They were the most consistent element of the ballgame. To hold an opponent like Colorado, with the kind of offense they have [40.3 points per game] to seven points is pretty significant."

The discrepancy was greater in the first half, when Nebraska outgained Colorado 234 yards to 89 to take a 17-0 lead, and the Cornhuskers wound up controlling the ball for 38 minutes 24 seconds.

Aside from a 41-yard sprint down the sideline, Nebraska pretty much kept the nation's leading rusher and Heisman Trophy candidate, Rashaan

I-back Lawrence Phillips rushed for 86 yards behind one of the most powerful offensive lines in the nation.

Abdul Muhammed races upfield after a reception.

105

Salaam, in check. Salaam gained 134 yards, 45 yards less than his average. In the first half, Colorado quarterback Kordell Stewart completed just 2-of-6 passes and star receiver Michael Westbrook had just one reception as the Buffaloes unexpectedly emphasized the running game.

"I was surprised," said Donta Jones, a Nebraska linebacker from La Plata, Md., who had seven tackles and a sack. "Colorado has been known as a passing team in the last couple years, but they came out and tried to run on us and we've got a great defense to stop the run." Stewart finished 12-for-28 for 150 yards and Westbrook had six catches for 80 yards.

The star quarterback was Nebraska's Brook Berringer, who was efficient if unspectacular. Berringer, playing his first full game since being sidelined with a collapsed lung on Oct. 1, completed 12-of-17 passes for 142 yards and a touchdown. His only major mistake came on an ill-advised pass in the third quarter, which Colorado cornerback Dalton Simmons intercepted for the game's only turnover.

About the only other thing that went wrong for Nebraska was the end of I-back Lawrence Phillips's string of 100-yard rushing games. He had topped 100 yards in every game this season and actually had more than 100 yards early in the third quarter, but fell to 86 yards on several negative-yardage plays, including a 17-yard loss on a bad pitch. Fullback Cory Schlesinger gained 65 yards.

The Cornhuskers dominated in field position even when they weren't scoring. They had three touchdowns and a field goal on their first six possessions and ended drives in Colorado territory when they didn't score. The Buffaloes had to start drives on their 3, 11, 8, and 7 and got their only touchdown after the interception gave them the ball on the Nebraska 36. Rashaan Salaam took in a

Terry Connealy (99) and Donta Jones (84) bring eventual Heisman winner Rashaan Salaam to his knees.

NEBRASKA VS. COLORADO

The grease on the goalposts made no difference to Nebraska fans, exultant after the 24–7 victory over rival Colorado.

six-yard run five plays later to make it 24-7 with 1:06 left in the third quarter, but Nebraska's play never left much room for hope that the Buffaloes would come back.

Overall, it was an inspired effort by a Nebraska team that has yearned for respect since starting quarterback Tommie Frazier was ruled out for the season because of a blood clot and the Cornhuskers began losing support in the polls. They knew they needed a strong performance in this nationally televised game against the No. 2 team to gain the favor of the voters.

"We looked at the big picture," Jones said. "That's one thing about Nebraska: We play in big games."

But they usually don't win them. This snapped a string of 12 consecutive defeats to top-five teams that dated to 1987. The Cornhuskers think that eliminating that reputation of losing the big one will help their cause of gaining the No. 1 ranking.

"It's a good argument," cornerback Barron Miles said. "A week ago [a 42-7 victory at Missouri] it was a good argument and the week before that [17-6 at Kansas State]. How many tests do you have to go through to get someone's attention?"

It didn't help that No. 1 Penn State clobbered Ohio State, 63-14, which might give the Cornhuskers reason to pay attention to another shirt slogan, one worn by several players after the game: "Unfinished business."

BUFFS SAY CORNHUSKERS DESERVE NO. 1

From The Associated Press

LINCOLN, Neb., Oct. 30, 1994—Brook Berringer silenced his doubters and Nebraska's defense silenced Colorado. The result was a loud Cornhuskers' claim that they deserve to be No. 1.

Berringer, thrust into the spotlight after starter Tommie Frazier was sidelined for the season, directed the offense with precision and the Cornhuskers shut down Colorado's high-powered attack yesterday for a 24-7 victory in their Big Eight showdown.

The win over the second-ranked Buffaloes (7-1, 3-1) gave the No. 3 Cornhuskers (9-0, 4-0) the inside track to the Big Eight championship and Orange Bowl berth, and could vault them over No. 1 Penn State when the polls are released today.

"In my mind, I think we're the No. 1 team in the country," linebacker Ed Stewart said. "We played a great team today and beat them soundly."

Penn State, meanwhile, did all it could to hold onto its top spot, trouncing No. 21 Ohio State 63-14.

"I don't want to get into that controversy," Nebraska Coach Tom Osborne said. "We'll let the pundits figure that out."

Penn State Coach Joe Paterno took the same tact.

"I don't see Tom Osborne arguing that his kids are No. 1 . . . and I don't see any reason I should," he said.

Colorado Coach Bill McCartney, whose team has beaten five ranked opponents this season, endorsed the Huskers:

"Nebraska is the best team we've played to date and I don't see any reason they shouldn't be No. 1. They dominated from the onset in all phases of the game."

Berringer was playing at full strength for the first time since suffering a partially collapsed lung against Wyoming on Oct. 1. Nebraska built a 24-0 lead on his 30-yard touchdown pass to tight end Eric Alford with 10:42 left in the third quarter.

Colorado, 0-for-11 on third down tries for the game, finally scored on Rashaan Salaam's six-yard run with 1:06 remaining in the third.

Salaam, the nation's leading rusher with a 179-yard average, gained 134 yards on 22 carries. But his only long run was a 41-yarder in the third quarter.

"I'm shocked and disappointed," he said. "We came in here confident and we couldn't get it done. . . . Tell Nebraska to take the national championship. They deserve it."

Nebraska 24
Colorado 7

Nebraska	7	10	7	0	– 24
Colorado	0	0	7	0	– 7

Neb—Schlesinger 14 run (Sieler kick)
Neb—FG Sieler 24
Neb—Childs 2 run (Sieler kick)
Neb—Alford 30 pass from Berringer (Sieler kick)
Col—Salaam 6 run (Voskeritchian kick)
A—76,131.

TEAM STATISTICS

Category	Neb	Col
First downs	20	18
Rushes-yards	53-203	37-155
Passing Yards	142	159
Return Yards	9	7
Passing	12-17-1	13-30-0
Punts	6-38	6-38
Fumbles-Lost	1-0	0-0
Penalties-Yards	6-41	4-30
Time of Possession	38:24	21:36

INDIVIDUAL STATISTICS

RUSHING: Nebraska—Phillips 25-86, Schlesinger 8-65, Makovicka 3-32, Berringer 7-19, Childs 5-14, Benning 3-1, Muhammad 1-1, team 1-(minus 15). Colorado—Salaam 22-134, Stewart 14-24, Troutman 1-(minus 3).
PASSING: Nebraska—Berringer 12-17-1-142. Colorado—Stewart 12-28-0-150, Detmer 1-2-0-9.
RECEIVING: Nebraska—Alford 5-78, Gilman 4-46, Muhammad 2-14, Phillips 1-4. Colorado—Westbrook 6-80, Lepsis 2-18, Carruth 2-28, Salaam 2-24, Savoy 1-9.

ASSOCIATED PRESS TOP 10

	Team	Rec.	Votes	LW
1.	Nebraska (33)	9-0-0	1,520	3
2.	Penn St. (28)	7-0-0	1,514	1
3.	Auburn (1)	8-0-0	1,427	4
4.	Florida	6-1-0	1,322	5
5.	Miami (Fla.)	6-1-0	1,267	6
6.	Alabama	8-0-0	1,221	8
7.	Colorado	7-1-0	1,214	2
8.	Florida St.	6-1-0	1,167	9
9.	Utah	8-0-0	1,033	NR
10.	Syracuse	6-1-0	892	NR

USA TODAY/CNN TOP 10

	Team	Rec.	Votes	LW
1.	Penn St. (32)	7-0-0	1,520	1
2.	Nebraska (30)	9-0-0	1,518	2
3.	Miami (Fla.)	6-1-0	1,373	4
4.	Alabama	8-0-0	1,358	5
5.	Florida	6-1-0	1,313	6
6.	Florida St.	6-1-0	1,251	7
7.	Colorado	7-1-0	1,189	3
8.	Utah	8-0-0	1,074	11
9.	Syracuse	6-1-0	1,014	12
10.	Virginia	6-1-0	896	16

BERRINGER GIVES HUSKERS SOME BREATHING ROOM

By MICHAEL WILBON
Washington Post

LINCOLN, Neb., Oct. 30, 1994—Just three weeks ago, it looked like the Nebraska Cornhuskers would be snapping the ball directly to the I-back. They were fresh out of quarterbacks. Their premier player, Tommie Frazier—maybe the best player on the team, the man who had won 20 of 23 consecutive starts—was out for the season with a second blood clot in his right leg. His backup, Brook Berringer, suffered a partially collapsed lung in consecutive games. A walk-on player, Matt Turman, went to the sideline the next week with a bruised shoulder. That elevated a freshman, Monte Christo, who was so shocked at being called upon, he couldn't find his mouthpiece. At this point, Tom Osborne's backups were a wingback, a converted receiver and a converted student manager.

A national championship was looking pretty remote, but the student manager came through. The kid's real name is Andy Kucera, but everybody knows him as "Rudy" because he came in to mop up in a 70-21 drubbing of Pacific. Some of us presumed Osborne's pursuit of an elusive national championship was shot before the real chase began. Some of us were wrong.

"After Tommie and Brook, we were scared and nervous," said Turner Gill, the former Huskers quarterback and now quarterbacks coach. "We had a safety and a wingback as backups."

Fortunately for Nebraska, a flak jacket, some common sense and Berringer's re-inflated right lung have reversed what seemed to be a bad situation. Saturday, against supposed championship contender Colorado, the Nebraska coaches could finally exhale and remove their hands from their eyes. They could breathe easy, because Berringer could too.

He completed 12-of-17 passes for 142 yards and a touchdown in Nebraska's 24-7 romp over stunningly overmatched Colorado. A second-half interception is the only thing that reduced Berringer's performance from near-perfect to efficient. If he can stay healthy through New Year's Day, the Cornhuskers should be looking at a national title shot in the Orange Bowl against the Miami Hurricanes.

Most teams lose one of the best quarterbacks in school history, they're looking for a life raft to cling to. Berringer so far has been more than just a fill-in. When Frazier's season ended after a 4-0 start, Berringer took the reins against Wyoming. Down 14-0, he suffered a 40 percent collapsed lung on a hit before halftime but played the rest of the game and led a desperate, come-from-behind victory. He started the next week against Oklahoma State, but a pre-scheduled halftime X-ray showed the lung had collapsed 20 percent again and the coaches yanked him. Turman, the walk-on, started the next week at Kansas State, but Berringer played some and convinced the coaches he was well enough to play last week against Missouri.

There were conditions. Wear a flak jacket, and don't run any option plays. Nebraska play football without the option? Osborne bit the bullet. If the kid tried to run the option and got crunched, a given when you run the option, the Huskers would be relying on Rudy to get them to the Orange Bowl. "The doctors told us, 'If you can get by for two weeks without him getting hit, he should be all right,' " Gill said. "The last two weeks were so stressful for the coaches. We decided, 'No option, period! We had to get healthy if we wanted this

Husker quarterback Brook Berringer was quietly effective as Tommie Frazier's replacement. Steady and underrated, he keyed critical wins over dangerous Wyoming and archrival Colorado.

team to ever go full throttle."

While the coaches concede they are a better team with Frazier, Gill said, "We're not far off with Brook."

What they've got is a 6-foot-4, 210-pound junior who runs a 4.7 second 40-yard dash (to Frazier's 4.68). "Tommie's quicker running the option," Gill said, "but we might throw more passes with Brook in there."

Other than a bad read on the interception, the coaches couldn't have asked any more of a quarterback, even the Heisman candidate. His performance and a virtual shutout pitched by the Nebraska defense meant that this week's game of the century was a total bust. By the time the 200th consecutive sellout crowd hit the streets, the only issues were whether or not third-ranked Nebraska deserved to jump ahead of No. 1 Penn State and whether any of three players in this game deserved legitimate Heisman consideration.

A lackluster second half by the Huskers, and a 63-14 victory for Penn State over No. 21 Ohio State dismissed that topic.

And if you hear anybody mention Colorado quarterback Kordell Stewart or Nebraska running back Lawrence Phillips as a Heisman candidate, turn the page or the channel immediately. Stewart is another Big Eight quarterback who can run well, but throw just a little. The offense, though it's the fault of the coaches and not the player, isn't remotely sophisticated. Phillips is a nice runner at best, but happens to be playing behind one of the best offensive lines in college football history. Gill said this line, anchored by 315-pound left tackle Rob Zatechka and left guard Joel Wilks, could wind up better than the one he ran behind that featured Outland Trophy winner Dean Steinkuhler and two-time Outland winner Dave Rimington. Still, Phillips (more than 1,300 yards) doesn't break off any long, breathtaking runs, the kind a back with his speed should when the line is opening holes the size of a small sedan.

The real talent appears to be Colorado junior tailback Rashaan Salaam, but 41 of his 134 yards on 22 carries came on one dash in the second half. When the game was on the line, Stewart and Salaam did nothing, although the Nebraska defense gets a lot of credit for that.

Ultimately, the people of Nebraska aren't going to give a hoot about the Heisman anyway. They've had a Heisman winner (Mike Rozier, 1983) since they won a national championship in 1971. The way to accomplish the latter is to get more of the kind of stellar defense that shut down Colorado and more of the kind of quarterback play from Berringer, who has saved a season for his team and provided the kind of inspirational leadership that earns respect, if not awards.

NEBRASKA, PENN ST. IN A SHOVING MATCH

By J.A. ADANDE
Washington Post

Nebraska Coach Tom Osborne's team has finally received its long-sought recognition from the media. Now he only has to convince his fellow coaches.

The Cornhuskers moved up two spots and bumped Penn State out of the No. 1 ranking in the Associated Press media poll, while Penn State barely maintained its lead over Nebraska in the CNN/USA Today coaches' poll.

"The thing that is important is we are in a position now that if we continue to play well, at least we will have some things in our own hands," Osborne told reporters in Lincoln yesterday. "You like to be in the position where you can play for the whole thing in the end, or at least have a chance to."

It's a switch in support from last year, when the coaches had Nebraska No. 1 and the media had the Cornhuskers behind Florida State in the final regular season polls. Florida State beat Nebraska, 18-16, in the Orange Bowl and won a consensus national championship.

In yesterday's AP poll, the Cornhuskers picked up nine additional first-place votes following their 24-7 victory over then-No. 2 Colorado, for a total of 33 first-place votes and 1,520 points. Penn State (7-0), which thrashed Ohio State, 63-14, also gained nine first-place votes, totaling 28, with 1,514 points. But it was not enough to hold off the groundswell of support for Nebraska (9-0).

"I think anytime you can defeat the number two team in the country by the margin that we did, you can gain some respect," defensive tackle Terry Connealy said. "And it sounds like we did."

Colorado's 16 first-place votes were up for grabs when the Buffaloes fell from the ranks of the unbeaten. In addition, two of the three people who had voted Auburn No. 1 last week changed their minds.

In the CNN/USA Today coaches' poll, Penn State led with 1,520 points, including 32 first-place votes. Nebraska had 1,518 points and 30 first-place votes.

"I think at the end of the year, after everyone's played all their games, if I feel [that we're No. 1], I'll say it," Penn State Coach Joe Paterno told the Associated Press. "I think you win it by playing the season out."

If the current rankings hold up, there could be two national champions decided in two bowl games on two coasts. Nebraska appears headed to the Big Eight championship and a trip to the Orange Bowl in Miami; if Penn State wins its remaining games, the Nittany Lions will play the Pacific-10 champion in the Rose Bowl in Pasadena, Calif.

Nebraska has a home game vs. Kansas (5-3) and finishes the regular season on the road at Iowa State (0-7-1) and Oklahoma (4-4). The remainder of Penn State's schedule features road games at Indiana (5-3) and Illinois (5-3) and home games against Northwestern (3-4-1) and Michigan State (3-5).

There's a growing opinion that an undefeated season by Nebraska with a bowl victory over Miami or Florida State would be more deserving of a national championship than an undefeated season by Penn State with a bowl victory against a team such as Oregon, which is currently tied for first place in the Pac-10 despite a 6-3 record. Perhaps that would be enough to swing enough coaches into Nebraska's favor and give them a No. 1 ranking in both polls.

That's the penalty the Big Ten could face for being on the outside of the bowl coalition. When the coalition formed three years ago with the intent to increase the possibility of a No. 1 vs. No. 2 matchup in a bowl game, the Big Ten decided to stick with tradition and the $6 million-per-team payout of the Rose Bowl.

It might come back to haunt the conference if the Nittany Lions don't get a chance to determine their own outcome in what could be the conference's first national championship since Ohio State won in 1968. Penn State, which became a full-fledged member of the Big Ten last season, won the national championship as an independent in 1982 and '86.

The Big Eight's previous championship came courtesy of Colorado, which captured the Associated Press title in 1990 while Georgia Tech won the coaches' poll. The polls also couldn't decide on a national championship the next year, when Miami won the AP poll and Washington won the coaches' poll.

With the way things have gone this season, there's no guarantee that Nebraska—which hasn't won a title since 1971—will retain its No. 1 ranking. The Cornhuskers have lost it once this season, though they have gone undefeated since they took the top spot from Florida Sept. 4.

Voters bailed out on them when starting quarterback Tommie Frazier was ruled out for the season because of a blood clot in his leg and the Huskers had dropped to No. 3 in last week's poll. Even the local newspapers—or "key publicity outlets," as they are called in the Nebraska media guide—picked Colorado to win Saturday. But the Cornhuskers apparently won over most of their critics.

"I think we came out and played a great game against a great football team," Nebraska linebacker Ed Stewart said. "We weren't expected to do this well. We showed a lot of people how good this football team really is."

NO. 1 DEBATE: POLLS PROVIDE SPLIT DECISION

By STEVE WIEBERG
USA TODAY

LINCOLN, Neb., Oct. 31, 1994—Some arguments are destined never to be settled.

Fenway or Wrigley? Coke or Pepsi? Boxers or briefs?

Penn State or Nebraska?

Battle lines for the next 64 days in college football have been drawn. A day after both extended unbeaten seasons—the Nittany Lions embarrassing Ohio State, the Cornhuskers dominating Colorado—they shared the top ranking in the polls Sunday.

Perhaps it's justice. "We're going to come out and play every week and see if anybody can beat us," says Nebraska lineman Zach Wiegert. But Penn State won't get that shot and the Huskers can't get at the Lions.

In separate conferences, playing separate schedules, headed for separate bowls, the two contenders won't get within 440 miles of each other between now and Jan. 3, when the season is ended and the national championship decided by ballot.

Odds that somebody else will step in and unscramble the picture, with an upset, seem slim.

Penn State's biggest remaining regular-season hurdle is Nov. 12 at Illinois, with the nation's fourth-best defense but also a loss at home to Purdue.

For Nebraska, there's the matter of its annual Friday-after-Thanksgiving showdown with Oklahoma. But the Sooners have lost three of their last four and threaten to throw coach Gary Gibbs into the unemployment line.

So the debate figures to carry into the bowls, where comparative matchups could make a difference.

What's likely to mean more to voters in the polls, the Huskers taking on now-No. 3-ranked Miami (Fla.) in the Orange—a home game for the once beaten Hurricanes—or Penn State playing now-No. 14 Washington State in the Rose? Worse, Washington State could slip in the Pacific 10, and the Nittany Lions could find themselves playing even more lighly regarded Oregon.

As Nebraska coach Tom Osborne notes, "It's public opinion." Who can predict?

What looms is the most impassioned who's No. 1-debate since 1991, when Miami and Washington finished perfect seasons in separate bowls (Orange and Rose). The final polls split, The Associated Press media favoring the 'Canes and USA TODAY/CNN coaches the Huskies.

"I will not lobby," Osborne says. "All we want to do is play well. And if people feel we deserve to be rated No. 1, great. If not, we've done all we can."

Says Penn State's Joe Paterno: "I don't see Tom Osborne arguing . . . and I don't see any reason I should."

Except on the field.

Nebraska was first to play its hand Saturday and laid down the equivalent of a straight. The Huskers won their fifth and biggest game since quarterback Tommie Frazier was lost to recurring blood clots in his leg, 24-7 against previously unbeaten No. 3 Colorado.

Penn State answered with an astounding 63-14 rout of then-No. 14 Ohio State.

The Nittany Lions have the glitzier numbers, averaging almost a third of a mile of offense a game and beating their opponents by an average of 33 points. The Huskers have had to play with more heart to overcome the loss of Frazier, triggerman fo their option offense, in late September.

"A lot of people asked me before the season, 'What's going to happen if you don't have Tommie Frazier?'" lineman Rob Zatechka says. "Now you know. We're 9-0."

It was backup Brook Berringer, in particular, who defied the gloom-and-doomers, passing for 142 yards and a touchdown and quarterbacking Nebraska to a 24-0 lead in the first 35 minutes.

Still, Nebraska's offense lists heavily to the run. Penn State's almost is perfectly balanced, as underscored by quarterback Kerry Collins' and tailback Ki-Jana Carter's emergence as Heisman Trophy contenders.

"It's very, very difficult for anybody to be playing better than either of those guys are playing," Paterno says in the wake of Saturday's runaway, in which Collins was 19-for-23 for 265 yards and two touchdowns and Carter ran for 137 yards and four TDs.

Collins, a fifth-year senior who has been drafted twice in baseball and is catching the eye of NFL scouts, is on a pace to break Jim McMahon's 1981 NCAA record for efficiency.

"This is as well as I've played and as good as I've felt," he says, "at any time in athletics."

But does Nebraska need offensive balance? Wiegert, Zatechka and the rest of a massive and agile offensive line is impressive by even the Huskers high standards, which is why they're rushing for almost 370 yards a game.

"They did at will whatever they wanted to," says Colorado tackle Darius Holland. "I watched films and told my friends, 'That offensive line is going to take over the game and, with Lawrence (Phillips) back there (at tailback), they are going to run over everybody they come to.' And that's what they did."

So did a quicker-than-ever defense, which didn't allow the Buffaloes to convert any of 15 third- and fourth-down situations and now has allowed three, six, seven and seven points in its last four games.

Saturday's win was the Huskers first against a higher-ranked opponent since the 1987 Sugar Bowl. Penn State, meanwhile, was knocking off the second of the only two teams to beat the Nittany Lions during their inaugural Big Ten season a year ago (Michigan and Ohio State).

Tit for tat. It might be that way for awhile.

CAMPAIGN FOR NO. 1

From The Associated Press

LINCOLN, Neb., Nov. 5, 1994—Brook Berringer has proved himself yet again as Nebraska's quarterback.

Even after directing Nebraska's 24-7 victory over powerful Colorado a week ago, Berringer's talents had been questioned. Colorado Coach Bill McCartney said Berringer, who stepped in when blood clots sidelined Tommie Frazier in late September, had to prove he could throw to wide receivers instead of just the tight ends.

Yesterday, the wideouts were busy. Berringer threw for two touchdowns and Lawrence Phillips ran for two as No. 1 Nebraska beat Kansas 45-17.

"I'm done proving myself so don't even ask," Berringer said. "Our game plan was formed around what Bill McCartney

Fullback Jeff Makovicka escapes the clutches of defensive end Kevin Kopp and takes the ball in 8 yards for Nebraska's first score of the second quarter.

NEBRASKA VS. KANSAS

Dwayne Harris (86), Terry Connealy (99), Christian Peter (55), Donta Jones (84) and other Nebraska Blackshirts shut down the Kansas running game and allowed only 8 pass completions.

119

NEBRASKA VS. KANSAS

After the Colorado game, Buffalo head coach Bill McCartney gave Brook Berringer some advice. "He said we had to throw to our wide receivers," Berringer said after the 45-17 victory over Kansas. "So that's what we did." Berringer earned 267 passing yards and a spot in the Nebraska record book.

said last week. We had to get the ball to the split ends, the receivers to prove ourselves, so that's what we did."

Berringer, who hit 13 of 18 passes, threw for 267 yards, the most for a Nebraska quarterback since David Humm's 267 against Missouri in 1972.

Nebraska (10-0, 5-0 Big Eight) also got its 10th-straight 100-yard effort from Phillips. The sophomore, held to 35 yards on 11 carries in the first half, finished with 153 on 21 tries with scoring runs of 4 and 22 yards.

NEBRASKA VS. KANSAS

Brenden Stai (66) watches as Lawrence Phillips (1) scrambles for one of his two touchdowns against the Jayhawks.

NEBRASKA VS. KANSAS

Cornerback Tyrone Williams intercepted an Asheiki Preston pass at Nebraska's 30-yard line, leading off a 3-play, 70-yard touchdown drive.

JOE MIXAN

122

NEBRASKA VS. KANSAS

I-back Damon Benning escaped four would-be tacklers before taking a shovel pass for 37-yard gain, setting up Jeff Makovicka's 8-yard TD run.

JOE MIXAN

With Kansas (5-4, 2-3) taking early aim on Phillips, Berringer went to the air, hitting 8-of-10 for 249 yards and two touchdowns by halftime. Reggie Baul hauled in a 51-yard scoring pass and another to Clester Johnson covered 64 yards.

NEBRASKA VS. KANSAS

Dwayne Harris (86) and Troy Dumas (4) sack Kansas QB Asheiki Preston, who totaled only 7 pass completions.

"They crowded the run so we thought we had to get them off our backs," Coach Tom Osborne said. "So we threw the ball deep more than usual today. They were supporting with the secondary very fast. As a result they were a little more vulnerable to the deep ball.

"I thought Brook threw the ball pretty well today. Up to the last three or four minutes, he played pretty much flawlessly."

Nebraska 45
Kansas 17

| Nebraska | 24 | 14 | 7 | 0 | – | 45 |
| Kansas | 3 | 7 | 0 | 7 | – | 17 |

Neb—FG 35 Sieler
Neb—Baul 51 pass from Berringer (Sieler kick)
Kan—FG 41 McCord
Neb—Phillips 4 run (Sieler kick)
Neb—Schlesinger 40 run (Sieler kick)
Neb—Makovicka 8 run (Sieler kick)
Kan—Henley 6 run (McCord kick)
Neb—Johnson 64 pass from Berringer (Sieler kick)
Neb—Phillips 22 run (Sieler kick)
Kan—L.T. Levine 1 run (McCord kick)
A—75,543.

TEAM STATISTICS

Category	Neb	Kan
First downs	24	12
Rushes-yards	49-336	45-141
Passing yards	267	129
Return yards	39	26
Passes	13-18-0	8-23-2
Punts	3-49	6-39
Fumbles-lost	2-1	2-0
Penalties-yards	4-26	2-11
Time of possession	28:44	31:16

INDIVIDUAL STATISTICS
RUSHING: Nebraska—Phillips 21-153, Schlesinger 4-49, Benning 6-45, Schuster 3-25, Alford 1-17, Childs 4-16, Davenport 2-15, Makovicka 3-14, Turman 1-3, Berringer 4-(minus 1). Kansas—Henley 16-86, Levine 13-42, Davis 1-13, Vann 5-5, Williams 2-1, Good 1-1, Preston 6-0, Smith 1-(minus 7).
PASSING: Nebraska—Berringer 13-18-0-267. Kansas—Preston 7-18-2-107, Williams 1-4-0-22, Henley 0-1-0-0.
RECEIVING: Nebraska—Baul 3-106, Johnson 1-64, Benning 1-37, Alford 1-28, Holbein 2-12, Phillips 4-11, Gilman 1-9. Kansas—Friday 4-60, Harris 1-43, Reed 1-10, Levine 1-8, Willeford 1-8.

ASSOCIATED PRESS TOP 10

	Team	Rec.	Votes	LW
1.	Nebraska (39)	10-0-0	1,525	1
2.	Penn St. (22)	8-0-0	1,507	2
3.	Auburn (1)	9-0-0	1,430	3
4.	Florida	7-1-0	1,321	4
5.	Miami (Fla.)	7-1-0	1,283	5
6.	Alabama	9-0-0	1,239	6
7.	Colorado	8-1-0	1,194	7
8.	Florida St.	7-1-0	1,163	8
9.	Texas A&M	8-0-1	1,016	11
10.	Colorado St.	8-1-0	846	14

USA TODAY/CNN TOP 10

	Team	Rec.	Votes	LW
1.	Nebraska (42)	10-0-0	1,530	2
2.	Penn St. (20)	8-0-0	1,503	1
3.	Miami (Fla.)	7-1-0	1,375	3
4.	Alabama	9-0-0	1,365	4
5.	Florida	7-1-0	1,322	5
6.	Florida St.	7-1-0	1,269	6
7.	Colorado	8-1-0	1,183	7
8.	Arizona	7-2-0	982	13
9.	Kansas State	6-2-0	897	15
10.	Colorado St.	8-1-0	810	11

HUSKERS DEFEAT IOWA ST., 28-12

From The Associated Press

> **Tackle Terry Connealy (99) joins an avalanche of Nebraska defenders to stop fullback Artis Garris (21). "When you play against these guys, you can't believe they haven't won a game," Connealy said. "And I'm not exaggerating." Nevertheless, the Huskers held the Cyclones to 62 rushing yards.**

AMES, Iowa, Nov. 12, 1994—Brook Berringer passed for a touchdown and set up the clinching score with a 28-yard run yesterday as No. 1-ranked Nebraska clinched an Orange Bowl berth and a share of the Big Eight title with a 28-12 win over Iowa State.

Nebraska (11-0, 6-0 Big Eight) led only 7-6 late in the first half and 14-12 in the fourth quarter before

NEBRASKA VS. IOWA STATE

▲ **Cyclone running back Troy Davis (28) is slammed by tackle Christian Peter (55), who was in on 9 tackles. Iowa State had averaged 422.5 yards of offense in their previous four games, but Nebraska's defense held them to a season-low 213 yards.**

finally subduing the Cyclones with fourth-quarter touchdown runs by Damon Benning and Lawrence Phillips. Phillips finished with 183 yards in 36 carries after being held to 30 yards in 15 first-half carries.

Iowa State (0-9-1, 0-5-1) trailed, 14-12, after halfback Calvin Branch beat defensive back Kareem Moss down the left sideline and caught Todd Doxzon's perfectly lofted pass for a 58-yard touchdown with 3:42 left in the third quarter.

Memories of Iowa State's 19-12 upset of Nebraska at Ames two years ago filled Cyclone Stadium, but Nebraska stopped Doxzon on a two-point conversion run and eventually put the game away.

Nebraska finally opened some breathing room after forcing Iowa State to punt from its 8-yard line and taking over at the Cyclones' 41. Berringer ran 28 yards to the Iowa State 6 three plays later. On the next play, Benning sped untouched up the middle into the end zone with 12:09 left.

A holding penalty erased Doxzon's 32-yard TD pass to Geoff Turner with 9:40 remaining, and the Cyclones eventually had to punt. Phillips then ran 62 yards to the Iowa State 5 before fumbling into the end zone, where Russell Johnson recovered to give the Cyclones another chance.

But Nebraska held and Phillips scored on a 21-yard run with 1:25 left.

◀ ....

Memories of Iowa State's upset of the Huskers two years ago caused Nebraska defensive coordinator Charlie McBride to lose some sleep. "This was my worst week," McBride said. "I've never woke up in the middle of the night and had negative thoughts like I had last night. I was worried about the fake punts and of every trick play." There were no Cyclone tricks, but McBride's Blackshirts did sack Iowa State quarterback Todd Doxzon six times for 33 yards in losses.

Nebraska 28
Iowa St. 12

Nebraska	7	7	0	14	– 28
Iowa St.	0	6	6	0	– 12

Neb—Phillips 1 run (Sieler kick)
Iowa—FG Stewart 35
Iowa—FG Stewart 37
Neb—Muhammad 38 pass from Berringer (Sieler kick)
Iowa—Branch 58 pass from Doxzon (run failed)
Neb—Benning 6 run (Sieler kick)
Neb—Phillips 21 run (Sieler kick)
A—45,186.

TEAM STATISTICS

Category	Neb	Iowa
First downs	21	11
Rushes-yards	56-285	43-62
Passing yards	193	151
Return yards	3	7
Passes	11-18-1	8-13-0
Punts	5-42	8-45
Fumbles-lost	2-1	1-0
Penalties-yards	5-55	5-50
Time of possession	33:35	26:25

INDIVIDUAL STATISTICS

RUSHING: Nebraska—Phillips 36-183, Berringer 9-61, Schlesinger 7-24, Childs 2-9, Benning 1-6, Makovicka 1-2. Iowa St.—Guggenheim 6-32, Davis 4-10, Knott 3-8, Garris 6-7, Doxzon 20-4, Turner 1-2, Branch 3-(minus 1).
PASSING: Nebraska—Berringer 11-18-1-193. Iowa St.—Doxzon 8-13-0-151.
RECEIVING: Nebraska—Phillips 4-40, Baul 3-49, Muhammad 2-52, Gilman 1-48, Alford 1-4. Iowa St.—Turner 3-31, Branch 2-63, Mhoon 2-20, Horacek 1-37.

ASSOCIATED PRESS TOP 10

	Team	Rec.	Votes	LW
1.	Nebraska (39)	11-0-0	1,527	1
2.	Penn St. (23)	9-0-0	1,509	2
3.	Florida	8-1-0	1,351	4
4.	Alabama	10-0-0	1,332	6
5.	Miami (Fla.)	8-1-0	1,285	5
6.	Auburn	9-0-1	1,240	3
7.	Colorado	9-1-0	1,237	7
8.	Florida St.	8-1-0	1,176	8
9.	Texas A&M	9-0-1	1,024	9
10.	Colorado St.	9-1-0	927	10

USA TODAY/CNN TOP 10

	Team	Rec.	Votes	LW
1.	Nebraska (41)	11-0-0	1,525	1
2.	Penn St. (21)	9-0-0	1,504	2
3.	Alabama	10-0-0	1,386	4
4.	Miami (Fla.)	8-1-0	1,339	3
5.	Florida	8-1-0	1,309	5
6.	Florida St.	8-1-0	1,254	6
7.	Colorado	9-1-0	1,209	7
8.	Kansas St.	7-2-0	985	9
9.	Oregon	8-3-0	983	11
10.	Colorado St.	9-1-0	916	10

NEBRASKA WINS WITH OFFENSE BELOW AVERAGE

By CHARLIE NOBLES
New York Times

NORMAN, Okla., Nov. 25, 1994—As Tom Osborne moved one victory from his first national title in 22 years as coach of Nebraska, he opened the door to a sizable quarterback controversy.

The No. 1-ranked Cornhuskers (12-0) struggled to a 13-3 victory over Oklahoma before 70,216—their seventh straight with Brook Berringer as the team's starting quarterback. Yet Osborne admitted "looking at Tommie a few times" when the game was tied 3-3 at halftime.

"Tommie" is Tommie Frazier, who has been sidelined since Sept. 24 with blood clots in his right leg. He was in uniform on the sideline today and never took his jacket off.

Osborne, though, said he definitely expects Frazier to be available for the Orange Bowl game on Jan. 1, probably against Miami.

"We're running pretty smoothly the way it is

Oklahoma cornerback Wendell Davis (28) and defensive lineman Baron Tanner (92) combine to slam Brook Berringer to the turf. Although Berringer led the Huskers to victory over Oklahoma, head coach Tom Osborne admitted "looking at Tommie [Frazier] a few times."

now, and we have a lot of chemistry," Berringer said in measured tones. "I would think he would stick with me but I don't know."

He completed 13 of 23 passes for 166 yards to lead the Huskers to their fourth consecutive Big Eight title and 25th consecutive regular-season victory.

Averaging 38.4 points, 358 rushing yards and 493.8 total yards coming into the game, Nebraska struggled early and often against an inspired Oklahoma defense. The Cornhuskers would up with 136 on the ground and 302 overall.

Berringer led the Huskers on scoring drives on their first two possessions of the second half against a fired up Oklahoma team that was playing its last game for Coach Gary Gibbs, who announced his resignation on Monday.

Perhaps the most spectacular play of the game came when Nebraska wingback Abdul Muhammad caught a 24-yard pass from Berringer that put the Huskers at the Oklahoma 15-yard line.

What made the play special is that Muhammad,

Lawrence Phillips (1) is tripped up by defensive end Cedrick Jones (57). The Sooner defense was the first to hold Phillips under 100 yards this season, stopping him at 50.

Linebacker Phil Ellis (41) pulls down Oklahoma tailback James Allen (25). The Husker defense held the Sooners' rushing to a dismal 108 yards.

a 160-pounder, took a vicious hit from 191-pound cornerback Larry Bush just as the ball arrived.

"Soon as I caught the ball, I locked it up, just like we're taught to do," he said. "I didn't even see the guy coming."

The drive stalled and the Huskers were forced to settle for a 26-yard field goal by Tom Sieler.

Muhammad also teamed up with Berringer on Nebraska's next series to produce the game's longest play, beating safety Maylon Wesley badly for a 44-yard completion.

That put the ball at the Oklahoma 13, and three plays later Berringer scored on a one-yard plunge. Thirteen minutes remained but clearly Sooner chances had faded.

Gibbs was sure his Sooners would play hard in this finale, but he wasn't so sure they would play well. Afterward, he said, "We knew the game had to be low-scoring and it was. It came down to a few good plays, and Nebraska is the team that made those plays."

At least Oklahoma (6-5) did something nobody else has been able to do this season. It became the first to hold Nebraska running back Lawrence Phillips under 100 yards rushing this season. Phillips would have broken the National Collegiate Athletic Association Division I-A record for consecutive 100-yard games.

"The story of the game was the two defenses," Osborne said. "We knew they'd be tough. We were hoping some misdirection would work, but it didn't."

"It was not comfortable—but they looked a lot better in the second half," said Ed Williamson, the Orange Bowl Committee's president.

Nebraska reached the Oklahoma 28-yard line on its second possession, but a Matt Turman run on a fake 46-yard field goal was stopped short of the first down. The next time the Huskers were in a similar position, on the ensuing drive, they happily settled for Darin Erstad's 46-yard field goal.

Meanwhile, the Sooner offense didn't begin to solve Nebraska's defense until the second quarter. Their initial drive of that quarter reached the Nebraska 16, but Scott Blanton's 33-yard field goal attempt was blocked by cornerback Barron Miles, his fourth of the season.

Two series later, aided by a 25-yard pass from Garrick McGee to split end Albert Hall, the Sooners reached the visitor's 8, where Blanton tied the

NEBRASKA VS. OKLAHOMA

Fullback Cory Schlesinger (40) is dragged down by defensive end Arthur Atkins (96). Nebraska ball carriers were up against an inspired Oklahoma defense, playing their last game for head coach Gary Gibbs.

▲ **Wingback Abdul Muhammed (27) made 5 catches for 98 yards, including the game's longest play, a 44-yard pass completion from Berringer that set up a touchdown three plays later.**

game at 3 with a 25-yard field goal. But that was as good as it got for Oklahoma on this day.

Afterward, the Huskers talked of facing Miami in the Orange Bowl. The Hurricanes must defeat Boston College on Saturday to qualify.

"We all want to play Miami," said offensive tackle Rob Zatechka. "The way we see it, if we go down there and beat Miami on their home field, that's gong to make it easier for voters to give us the national championship."

Added Berringer: "We think we're the type of team that doesn't need to be on our home field to play well."

Nebraska 13
Oklahoma 3

| Nebraska | 0 | 3 | 3 | 7 | – | 13 |
| Oklahoma | 0 | 3 | 0 | 0 | – | 3 |

Neb—FG Erstad 46
OKL—FG Blanton 25
Neb—FG Sieler 26
Neb—Berringer 1 run (Sieler kick)
A—70,216

TEAM STATISTICS

Category	Neb	Okla
First downs	18	10
Rushes-yards	50-136	32-108
Passing yards	166	71
Return yards	0	20
Passes	13-23-1	6-18-2
Punts	5-47	7-38
Fumbles-lost	2-0	0-0
Penalties-yards	4-28	5-35
Time of possession	36:48	23:12

INDIVIDUAL STATISTICS

RUSHING: Nebraska—Phillips 21-50, Berringer 15-48, Benning 3-10, Schlesinger 3-11, Turman 1-9, Makovicka 3-9, Childs 3-6, Muhammad 1-(minus 7). Oklahoma—Moore 15-171, McGee 5-20, Allen 9-8, Chandler 3-9.

PASSING: Nebraska—Berringer 13-23-1-166. Oklahoma—McGee 6-17-2-71, Brown 0-1-0-0.

RECEIVING: Nebraska—Muhammad 5-98, Phillips 3-24, Gilman 2-23, Alford 2-16, Baul 1-5. Oklahoma—Hall 3-51, McDaniel 2-11, Allen 1-9.

ASSOCIATED PRESS TOP 10

	Team	Rec.	Votes	LW
1.	Nebraska (38)	12-0-0	1,523	1
2.	Penn St. (23)	11-0-0	1,509	2
3.	Alabama (1)	11-0-0	1,426	3
4.	Miami (Fla.)	10-1-0	1,346	5
5.	Colorado	10-1-0	1,308	6
6.	Florida	9-1-1	1,209	4
7.	Florida St.	9-1-1	1,186	7
8.	Texas A&M	10-0-1	1,095	8
9.	Auburn	9-1-1	1,057	9
10.	Colorado St.	10-1-0	969	10

USA TODAY/CNN TOP 10

	Team	Rec.	Votes	LW
1.	Nebraska (44)	12-0-0	1,531	1
2.	Penn St (18)	11-0-0	1,502	2
3.	Alabama	11-0-0	1,424	3
4.	Miami (Fla.)	10-1-0	1,351	5
5.	Colorado	10-1-0	1,277	7
6.	Florida	9-1-1	1,242	4
7.	Florida St.	9-1-1	1,211	6
8.	Kansas St.	9-2-0	1,077	8
9.	Oregon	9-3-0	1,028	9
10.	Colorado St.	10-1-0	987	10

SO MUCH PERFECTION. SO, WHO'S THE COLLEGE CHAMPION?

By MALCOLM MORAN
New York Times

UNIVERSITY PARK, Pa., Nov. 27, 1994—You are from Penn State, and you have every answer you need to know that the Nittany Lions have earned the right to play for a national championship in the Rose Bowl.

You are from Nebraska, and your conviction is inspired by the way the Cornhuskers dealt with the loss of quarterback Tommie Frazier to take a perfect record into the Orange Bowl.

You are from Alabama, and one step from the Sugar Bowl, all your team has done is beat everybody. Including Auburn. Thank goodness. Roll Tide.

You are from none of these places, but with the bowls weeks away you are already getting a New Year's headache just thinking about the resolution of a season that has been as confusing as it has been passionate.

The complex relationship between the polls and bowls has created the chaotic potential for an unprecedented January scenario of a three-headed monster, three national contenders whose perfect seasons end with bowl-game victories. The possibility of a three-way dispute, with polls of news media members and coaches then left to define degrees of perfection, has already revived calls for the National Collegiate Athletic Association to establish a football playoff for its major colleges, a call that has been made in the Nittany Valley since before Coach Joe Paterno's current players were born.

Bucky Greeley, the center Paterno calls Professor Greeley, was asked if he would want to play Nebraska.

"Not to be cocky or anything," Greeley said, "but I wish we could play them, and I think the Nebraska team would want to play us. Just to finally settle this."

"This" is the growing possibility of the sport's fourth controversial finish in five seasons. Last year, the issue was the lack of significance applied to Notre Dame's regular-season victory over Florida State when the Seminoles won the championship vote. In 1991, Miami and Washington took No. 1 rankings to opposite ends of the country. In 1990, Colorado and Georgia Tech were considered co-champions.

Now this. Kerry Collins, the quarterback of the Nittany Lions, said he would be eager to take on the demands of a four-team playoff that could lengthen his team's schedule by two games following the New Year's bowls.

"Win or lose," Collins said, "at least it would be decided the way it should be decided, on the field. I think anyone from Nebraska would tell you that. I think anyone from Penn State would tell you that. I think anyone from Alabama would tell you that. It just seems like a major shortcoming in college football. It's decided by people who have nothing to do with what goes on. That's a real shame."

The political structure is a particularly sensitive issue here, where Paterno's Lions saw perfect seasons end without championships in 1968, 1969 and 1973 and now face that empty happiness a fourth time.

Three weekends ago, Penn State was dropped to second behind Nebraska in the USA Today/CNN poll of coaches following a victory at Indiana, in which a 21-point lead was reduced to 6 in the final 1 minute 49 seconds—including a 2-point conversion with no time left—as many of the Lion starters watched from the sideline.

Nebraska's unexpectedly close 13-3 victory at Oklahoma last Friday did not lead to a comparable decline, despite the fact that the Huskers were in greater danger of losing than Penn State was at Indiana. The Cornhuskers gained 5 first-place votes, and 9 points for a 29-point lead in the poll of coaches. In The Associated Press writers' poll, Nebraska lost 1 first-place vote and 5 points to hold a 14-point lead.

In The New York Times computer ranking, Nebraska's small lead of .014 could be traced to two factors: a slightly better performance by its opponents, and an appearance in the Kickoff Classic that gave the Huskers one more victory than Penn State.

Since the 1969 season, when the A.P. poll established a permanent final result following bowl games, there have been just two years, 1969 and 1973, in which a pair of highly ranked teams ended perfect records with bowl-game victories. Each time, Penn State failed to gain the top spot.

Two factors could eventually create an orderly finish this time. To reach the Sugar Bowl, Alabama must defeat Florida on Saturday in the Southeastern Conference championship game. Nebraska is expected to face Miami in the Orange Bowl, where the Hurricanes have won 62 of their last 63 games after their 23-7 victory over Boston College on Saturday night.

Collins conceded that even with a Penn State victory over Oregon at Pasadena, Calif., on Jan. 2, a Nebraska victory the night before would be difficult to overcome.

Paterno and Nebraska Coach Tom Osborne, in their decisions this past weekend, each made a move that a cynic could interpret to be not-so-subtle election tactics. The Cornhuskers chose not to attempt a 30-yard field goal near the end of the game, opting for Brook Berringer's fourth-and-9 pass from the 13-yard line that was intercepted on the Oklahoma goal line.

And Penn State's final touchdown in a 59-31 victory over Michigan State resulted, Paterno said, from a plea by his players to allow running back Ki-Jana Carter to gain more than 200 yards.

ASSOCIATED PRESS TOP 10

	Team	Rec.	Votes	LW
1.	Nebraska (38)	12-0-0	1,526	1
2.	Penn St. (24)	11-0-0	1,511	2
3.	Miami (Fla.)	10-1-0	1,398	4
4.	Colorado	10-1-0	1,345	5
5.	Florida	10-1-1	1,345	6
6.	Alabama	11-1-0	1,217	3
7.	Florida St.	9-1-1	1,211	7
8.	Texas A&M	10-0-1	1,081	8
9.	Auburn	9-1-1	1,059	9
10.	Colorado St.	10-1-0	968	10

USA TODAY/CNN TOP 10

	Team	Rec.	Votes	LW
1.	Nebraska (44)	12-0-0	1,532	1
2.	Penn St. (18)	11-0-0	1,505	2
3.	Miami (Fla.)	10-1-0	1,406	4
4.	Florida	10-1-1	1,325	6
5.	Colorado	10-1-0	1,317	5
6.	Alabama	11-1-0	1,235	3
7.	Florida St.	9-1-1	1,218	7
8.	Kansas St.	9-2-0	1,076	8
9.	Oregon	9-3-0	1,051	9
10.	Colorado St.	10-1-0	976	10

BOWL COALITION POLL TOP 10

	Bowl coalition	Rec.	USA TODAY	AP
1.	Nebraska	12-0-0	1	1
2.	Penn St.	11-0-0	2	2
3.	Miami (Fla.)	10-1-0	3	3
4.	Colorado	10-1-0	5	4
5.	Florida	10-1-1	4	5
6.	Alabama	11-1-0	6	6
7.	Florida St.	9-1-1	7	7
8.	Texas A&M	10-0-1	NE	8
9.	Auburn	9-1-1	NE	9
10.	Kansas St.	9-2-0	8	11

THE SILENT PLAINSMAN

By STEVE MARANTZ
The Sporting News

LINCOLN, Neb., Dec. 19, 1994—Tom Osborne is a man hard to know, as near and as far as a prairie horizon.

A few years ago, after Nebraska's spring intrasquad game, Osborne and his top defensive coach, Charlie McBride, went fishing. Jumped in Osborne's car and made a beeline from Lincoln toward Valentine, hard by the Snake River. Problem was, Osborne's foot got a little heavy and an officer flagged him just past Long Pine. Another speeding ticket wasn't the end of the world—there have been a few—but it so happened a gust of wind blew Osborne's license out of the officer's hand. Osborne muttered a "dadgummit" under his breath while he politely assisted the officer and McBride in a search for the license. Problem was, it was dark and cold, and in Osborne's imagination, plump, high-colored trout were calling to him.

By the time they found the license, and the horrified officer apologized profusely as he wrote the citation—of all the lousy luck, to stop the head coach—Osborne's mind was miles up the highway, on the river. A while later, at 2:30 a.m., Osborne braked near to the river and said it was time to sleep, and three hours later, at dawn, he shook the slumbering McBride. Holding his gear, Osborne pointed up the river. "I'm going this way," he said. Then Osborne pointed down the river. "You go that way."

Perhaps you have to be a Nebraskan to fully appreciate Osborne. Same as you have to be a rural Nebraskan to love the wide empty spaces, the endless wind and sky. Same as you have to be an Omahan to know that from the long spine of Dodge Street radiates a graceful and garrulous urbanity.

Nebraska is not too far past its frontier beginnings, a time when the Union Pacific chose the banks of the Missouri River as the place to commence connecting America by track. Somehow, miraculously, the railroad never brought with it the cynical warp of life on the coasts. Nebraskans believe they inhabit Canaan on the prairie, a place where hard work and honesty are rewarded with milk, honey and victories over Colorado and Oklahoma.

Osborne embodies the best of Nebraska's self-image. He is upright, modest and courteous. Behind his outward gentleness is a backbone of iron; inside his reticence is a personality shrewd and droll.

Osborne fits a heroic Western archetype: the silent plainsman. Tall, lean and laconic. If you've seen "The Virginian" and "High Noon," you've seen Osborne. Gary Cooper plays him.

"I've often thought that Tom belongs to a generation gone by—from a time when the West was won," says Nancy Osborne, his wife of 32 years and mother of their three grown children. "There was a time when a handshake meant a deal was done, when a man was measured by his actions, not by what he said. Tom doesn't say much, but when he does, he really has something to say.

"His type is so out of the ordinary for this day and age that people misunderstand it, especially the press."

"Are you saying that your husband is out of time?" I ask.

"No, because that sounds like something is wrong with him," Nancy Osborne says. "I just mean there aren't a whole lot of people anymore who let their actions speak for them."

Osborne published his autobiography, "More Than Winning," in 1985, an astonishing act of self-revelation roughly equivalent to a cloistered monk singing "Stairway to Heaven" on primetime Husker Vision.

In it, Osborne lays out his philosophy of coaching, a high-minded approach emphasizing "process" over results. Osborne's model casts himself as a teacher-mechanic who nurtures young minds and bodies as he assembles them piece by piece into a purring engine.

The way Osborne tells it, he experienced an epiphany as an assistant coach under Bob Devaney, after Nebraska clinched the 1971 national title by routing Alabama in the Orange Bowl.

He writes: "The important thing about athletics really is the process. It's the path you follow in attempting to win the championship that's important. The relationships that are formed. The effort given. The experiences you have. And when it's over, it's all over! Everything else, at least for me, was kind of anticlimax."

Osborne also writes of the unsettling effect of World War II on his childhood. Osborne was 4 when his father, Charles, went off to fight, and 9 when he returned. During those years, Osborne, his younger brother, Jack, and his mother lived with his mother's parents in St. Paul, Neb. His grandparents had lost two farms during the Great Depression.

There was a feeling, Osborne writes, "of being from the wrong side of the tracks, which resulted from the absence of my father and the uncertainty of wartime. Much of my life has been directed toward proving something—what it is I don't really know—but the roots of that striving, I am sure, lie in the events surrounding my childhood experiences during World War II."

Introverted, Osborne channeled his emotions into sports. He was a standout in football, basketball and track, at Hastings (Neb.) High School and at tiny Hastings College. After college, Osborne made the San Francisco 49ers' taxi squad as an 18th-round draft choice. He was traded to the Washington Redskins, for whom he made 31 receptions in two seasons.

But Osborne saw that his playing future was limited, so he moved back to Nebraska to pursue a graduate degree in educational psychology.

In the early 1960s, Nebraska was emerging as a national power under Devaney. Osborne was attracted by the rising heat of his program.

Devaney was attracted by Osborne's keen grasp of offensive football.

Devaney, a puckish denizen of the night, hired Osborne, a teetotaling churchgoer. Somehow, they fit.

Osborne surveyed his new profession and saw nomads, flotsam and dreamers. He writes of his reservations: "The only way I want to stay in this for any length of time, I thought, is if I can be a head football coach where I can take control of my destiny."

Until Devaney's retirement in 1972, Osborne was his offensive mastermind. He persuaded Devaney to adopt a balanced-line I-formation attack that fueled national championships in 1970 and '71.

The '71 team, perhaps the best college team ever, featured junior wingback Johnny Rodgers, perhaps the best offensive player ever. When Nebraska drove 74 yards to score late on Thanksgiving Day 1971 to beat second-ranked Oklahoma, 35-31, in perhaps the greatest college football game ever, Osborne sent down the plays.

After the '72 season—after Devaney coached his last game and Rodgers played his last game—the man chosen to carry on their legacy was Osborne. He was 35 and, he supposed, in control of his destiny.

Since 1973, Osborne-coached teams have won 218 games and 11 Big Eight titles. They never have won fewer than nine games. Osborne's career victories rank third behind Joe Paterno and Bobby Bowden among active Division I-A coaches, and eighth all time.

Nebraska's success is based on the autonomy and loyalty of Osborne's assistant coaches; academic and spiritual encouragement, combined with a frank and respectful approach, to players; rehabilitative rather than punitive discipline; and abundant material resources. It also feeds off Osborne's perspective.

"I think if you look at me, I try not to overreact," he says. "Sometimes when you lose a game or two, you can start a downward spiral by blaming people—or changing. You can start losing games you ought to win. I try to maintain a consistent approach whether we win or lose.

"I try to be thorough. There are no real geniuses in this business. If you do your homework and get the right kind of players and coaches, you're going to come out on top but not always win. You've got to understand that."

Despite a variety of minor infractions, incidents of aberrant player behavior, a lower-than-average graduation rate among black players until recent years, intimations of steroid abuse and a full-bore NCAA investigation in 1986 that turned up passgate violations, Nebraska's reputation remains relatively spotless.

Its foundation is Osborne's integrity.

"I picked Nebraska because people told me Tom Osborne was somebody you could trust," says Turner Gill, quarterback from 1981 through '83, now the quarterbacks coach.

But . . . Three seasons—1981, 1983 and 1993— his teams could have won national championships by winning the Orange Bowl.

The '83 team could have won the title by kicking an extra point to tie Miami in the final seconds. Instead, it failed on a two-point attempt and Miami was champion. The two-point decision remains Osborne's finest moment on the national stage. Nonetheless, it was a loss.

Three other years—1975, 1984 and 1987—the Cornhuskers needed only to beat Oklahoma to take a No. 1 or No. 2 ranking into the Orange Bowl. They didn't. In the 1970s, Osborne was 1-6 against Oklahoma.

Osborne's 8-13 bowl record (including 0-7 the past seven seasons) and 2-9 record against Florida teams since 1980 complete the picture.

Last January 1 in the Orange Bowl, Nebraska outplayed 17½-point favorite Florida State. The lead changed five times, but the last belonged to FSU on a 22-yard field goal with 21 seconds left. FSU won the game, 18-16, and the national title. Nebraska won a moral victory.

If Osborne was disappointed, he barely showed it. Bad result, good process.

But the loss, fitting the larger pattern of Osborne's career, begged a question. Is Osborne's preoccupation with "process" a rationalization of his repeated frustration with results?

Further, does emphasizing process elevate form over function, and conveniently, justify losing? Can comfort with losing prefigure it at the highest level of football, where a winning edge may be as thin as a philosophical splitting of hairs? Does emphasis on process result in "processed" performance, well-drilled and methodical, but lacking in emotion, spontaneity and creativity?

It would be incomplete to portray Osborne as a Marlboro Man without lung cancer. He also is a kinder, gentler Newt Gingrich, equal parts political and spiritual.

Politically, Osborne usually is sticking his nose, albeit ineffectively, into an issue at the conference, CFA or NCAA level. He has campaigned for player stipends and liberal walk-on rules, and against scholarship reduction and Proposition 12, which stiffens academic requirements. He lost his effort to ensure that Nebraska play arch-rival Oklahoma yearly under Big Eight/12 realignment.

Spiritually, Osborne is a devout Methodist and reformist Christian who believes society needs a return to religious values. He draws his opinions from the books of Charles Colson, the Watergate felon who has built a second career as a born-again Christian advocating welfare reform, a reinvigorated work ethic, inmate rehabilitation and economic markets free of government regulation. For years, Colson's followers were marginalized as a fringe. The ascendance of Gingrich and the Christian Right suddenly makes Colson's message mainstream.

Osborne does not flaunt his piety, although occasionally it gets the better of him. He is careful not to alienate supporters—particularly Omaha's influential Jewish community—with a strong Christian or rightwing political message. But he is there alongside Colson, quietly searching for a spiritual solution to that which ails America.

"A lot of the cultural breakdown Colson writes about, I see the results of on my football team," Osborne says.

"Coaching is a way different animal now than it was 20 years ago—it's disturbing. Anymore, coaching 70 percent of the time is putting out brush fires, things that don't have anything to do with football. Players bring so much baggage with them, family difficulties, societal difficulties. We have several kids on our team who essentially have no parents and haven't had parental support since they were 10, 11 years old.

"I think of the cultural environment—the messages kids get from TV and some of the music they listen to—nobody is impervious to constant hammering of certain themes and messages. It makes it more difficult to coach."

Occasionally, Osborne's values place him in a quandary. Last January, junior cornerback Tyrone Williams was accused of shooting at a car. Two felony charges are pending. Williams, raised in a Florida project by a grandmother no longer able to care for him, is the kind of youth for whom Osborne professes concern. Such youths, Osborne believes, need extra patience and nurturing.

Osborne suspended Williams from the spring game and the first game of 1994, but he resisted suggestions to take stronger action. He says he will reconsider Williams' situation pending the outcome of his trial in January. By that time, Osborne will have benefited from Williams' sizable talent through most of a season. In being fair to Williams, Osborne is being fair to himself.

Osborne is active in the Fellowship of Christian Athletes, teaches Sunday school and supports up-from-poverty self-help causes. But he wants to do more.

When Nebraskans wonder how much longer Osborne plans to bless them with Saturday-afternoon nirvana, the answer probably lies in his restless spiritual quest. Three years ago, Osborne named Frank Solich as assistant head coach, a move thought to be the first transition step. About that time, boosters noticed Osborne pulling back from public events.

It cannot be easy for so private a man to live in so public a position. On the Sunday morning after Nebraska's season-making victory over Colorado, Osborne attended St. Mark's Methodist Church in Lincoln. At the start of the service, Pastor Cecil Bliss, a longtime friend, congratulated Osborne and a couple of his assistants seated among the congregants.

"Let's give them a round of applause," Bliss said. "We're very proud of them. They're loyal to church and community."

The congregation applauded. Bliss then asked if any among the 1,800 congregants had missed the game. Not a hand was raised.

Second to Jesus, fishing is Osborne's salvation. Osborne likes nothing more than fishing, except maybe silence. Fishing is his escape.

Osborne has dropped lines from Alaska to the Great Lakes. A 31-pound Chinook salmon taken from Lake Michigan is mounted on one office wall, a rainbow trout from Wyoming on another. In the 1970s, he twice considered other head-coaching jobs—Colorado and the Seattle Seahawks—mainly because of fishing opportunities. Now, a stocked pond behind his Lincoln home allows for occasional in-season reverie. Says friend Woody Varner: "Tom can throw his line out and spell his name with it."

"Is fishing a metaphor for football?" I ask Osborne.

He chews on the idea. Eventually he says, "I guess fishing is about winning, and somehow if you can entice the fish to bite you've won. I don't care about bringing home a bunch of fish. It's more the pursuit of the fish, getting it to hit the fly or whatever. Dealing with nature is challenging. There are so many different weather variables, stream variables, that you figure every day is different.

"Football is a little that way, too. You go out on the field and you don't know how they're going to defend you, or what's going to come up in the course of a game. There are very few predictable elements.

"But, basically, I use fishing as a diversion. When you play golf, there's usually somebody with you that wants to talk about football. Football comes up in so many social activities. Fishing, I'm quite often solitary. Most of the people I fish with don't talk about football."

But doesn't fishing require patience, same as coaching football, I ask. Osborne begins to suspect where this is headed.

"I think I've got a fair amount of patience," Osborne says. "Also, I guess if your object is to put a fish in the boat, you have to wait a long time. When I'm fishing I'm always active, casting the fly or lure, there's a lot of action. A lot of people get exasperated if they don't catch a fish. To me the actual process of fishing is important. Whether I catch a fish or not, I enjoy what I'm doing."

Any big ones get away, I ask. Osborne's suspicions are confirmed. He grins faintly.

"Maybe a few in football," he says. "But not fishing."

"I've got a surprise for you," I say. "No national championship questions."

"Good," Osborne says. "I don't mind."

Nancy Osborne speaks for herself and her husband on the question of a national championship.

"We've been so close so many times that in our hearts we know the kids did it," she says. "Having experienced that makes you focus on the importance of self-satisfaction. You don't let it destroy your lives if you don't win it."

She laughs. "Thank God," Nancy says. "Or we'd have been destroyed three times."

Osborne professes indifference to the rankings, but he cannot rationalize away their universal appeal. At the start of the season, Osborne stood before a blackboard and asked players to list goals. One raised his hand and said, "Win the national championship." Osborne dutifully chalked it up.

"He never says anything about a national championship, but I think he cares," senior linebacker Ed Stewart says. "It would be really special for the team if we were able to win one for him."

History honors champions. Fair or not, posterity will know Osborne as "durable, consistent, weak finisher" unless he gets it done.

"Tom is the finest coach in the country, but he's got that one point to prove—going all the way," says Devaney, athletic director emeritus. "It's the thing that keeps him from being recognized in the overall era of great coaches."

Osborne may accept this implicitly. At an age—57—when most coaches are worn out, Osborne seems to be getting better, cagier, more adaptable. His focus suggests a profound motivation.

Coaches and players credit him with pulling the team through a three-week period when the top two quarterbacks were injured. Against Colorado, Osborne might have called his best game.

"When Tom came up with his concept in the Colorado game, you could see he could be as good as he wanted to be," says Rodgers.

When Osborne became Nebraska's head coach in 1973—America still was in Vietnam and telephones were answered by people—he saw it as a chance to control his destiny. To a certain extent, he was prophetic. But Osborne also knows, almost 22 years later, that destiny, like a football, bounces with maddening impunity.

Now Osborne faces Miami, deja vu, in the Orange Bowl. A victory makes him coach of the national champion. A victory takes the air out of destiny's bounce. A victory enables Osborne to say, finally, "Good process good result."

HUSKERS MAKING ONE MORE OB RUN

By SUSAN MILLER DEGNAN
Miami Herald

MIAMI, Jan. 1, 1995—The bright red letters atop the University of Nebraska media guide for tonight's FedEx Orange Bowl say this:

UNFINISHED BUSINESS.

After seven consecutive bowl-game losses and 13 of 21 postseason losses since Tom Osborne became the head coach in 1973, the Huskers are seeking closure to this postseason frustration—especially since tonight's game against University of Miami marks the end of the Big Eight Conference's 20-year affiliation with the Orange Bowl.

Chances are the next year, with the new college football Bowl Alliance in place, the Huskers will be in another city come bowl time.

"We haven't set the world on fire certainly the last seven, and I don't remember any that we've been favored in, either," Osborne said. "We played well enough to win last year [18-16 Florida State victory]. And two years ago, even though the score was a 13-point difference [27-14 FSU victory], I thought we played Florida State fairly evenly.

"The main thing in winning a bowl game is just having a better football team."

To beat third-ranked Miami (10-10), the top-ranked Cornhuskers (12-0) must first and foremost do what they do best: run.

In 1994, Nebraska earned its 11th NCAA rushing title, averaging 340 yards per game. It was the ninth title in the past 15 years, and the 17th time in 18 years that NU has rushed for more than 300 yards a game. The Huskers ranked fifth in total offense, averaging 477.8 yards a game.

Miami's defense ranked seventh nationally against the run (allowing 96.8 yards a game) and first overall (220.9 yards a game) and first overall (220.9 yards a game) and in points allowed (10.8 a game).

"It's as quick as any team we've seen," said Osborne, whose teams traditionally throw once for every three to four running plays.

If Nebraska is to penetrate Miami's defense, Outland Trophy winner Zach Wiegert—an offensive tackle—will have to work even harder than usual. Wiegert will line up across from UM defensive end Kenny Holmes. Warren Sapp, winner of the Lombardi Trophy, plays on the other side.

"I've watched them in films, and they move real well," said Wiegert, a 6-5 300-pound senior. "But the thing they do that's most important of all—and doesn't get noticed—is make a lot of their tackles from the back side of the line.

"A lot of times, offensive linemen get lazy on the back side of the play. There will be no time to rest in this game."

HUSKERS HARVEST A DREAM

By AMY NIEDZIELKA
Miami Herald

MIAMI, Jan. 1, 1995—The celebration lasted longer than the surge.

The University of Nebraska football team spent 20 minutes on the field, cheering its national championship Sunday night after scoring 15 points in a thrilling final 15 minutes to defeat Miami, 24-17, in the FedEx Orange Bowl.

The Cornhuskers' victory in front of 81,753 ended a bowl victory drought of seven years.

"It's a great way to close it out, to play Miami in Miami and finally beat them," Nebraska Coach Tom Osborne said. "We've had a terrible time with these folks."

Nebraska scored two touchdowns in the fourth quarter to take the game away from Miami (10-2), which has lost three straight New Year's Day games. Nebraska's victory renders almost meaningless today's Rose Bowl game between No. 2 Penn State and Oregon.

"We'll have to see what happens on the vote," Osborne said. "If they give it to us, we will certainly be grateful. We'll take it home."

Nebraska (13-0), the top-ranked team going into the game, will almost undoubtedly be voted national champions when the polls are released Tuesday morning, giving Osborne his first title in 22 years. The victory ended Nebraska's string of failures in the Orange Bowl—the Huskers had lost five times there with no victories since 1984, including three losses to the Hurricanes.

"The Orange Bowl has been tremendous to us," Osborne said. "If there have been some problems, it's mainly that we haven't won down here enough."

The winning touchdown came with 2:46 remaining in the game. Nebraska fullback Cory Schlesinger ran up the middle for 14 yards to score his second touchdown of the game—and the fourth quarter.

Schlesinger ran right past Warren Sapp, who thought the hand-off was going to I-back Lawrence

Tommie Frazier, out since September with blood clots behind his right knee, returned to Orange Bowl action in the final quarter, igniting the Huskers to scoring drives of 40 and 58 yards to secure the national championship for Nebraska, its first national crown since 1971.

THE ORANGE BOWL: NEBRASKA VS. MIAMI

Phillips. Schlesinger reached the end zone almost untouched. The run completed a seven-play, 58-yard drive that took 3:42.

It also completed a remarkable comeback by Nebraska.

Just when it looked like Miami had the game wrapped up, the Huskers scored in stunning fashion. A 15-yard touchdown run by Schlesinger followed a 25-yard run by Phillips. Those runs represented Nebraska's entire scoring drive. It took just 33 seconds.

And when Tommie Frazier, who was named Nebraska's Most Valuable Player, hit tight end Eric Alford in the back of the end zone for the two-point conversion, the score was suddenly tied, 17-all, with 7:38 remaining.

The game took a turn for the bizarre early in the fourth quarter.

After an unsuccessful Miami drive, a high snap from Jeff Taylor on a punt attempt sent punter Dane Prewitt scurrying toward the end zone. Rather than allowing Nebraska to pick up the loose ball, Prewitt soccer-kicked the ball out of the end zone.

He was charged with an illegal kick, and Nebraska was awarded a first and goal from Miami's four. (The full explanation: Miami was assessed a four-yard penalty with a loss of down and a "team rushing loss" of 35 yards.)

A surprising call followed. Nebraska, the nation's leading rushing offense (340 yards per game), tried to pass. Safety Earl Little made a leaping interception of a Brook Berringer pass in the end zone, preserving Miami's 17-9 lead.

Miami scored just over a minute into the second half. By this time, Miami's offensive game plan was clear: the Hurricanes wanted quick, blitz-beating completions to their speedy receivers. After that, it was up to the receiver to outmaneuver Nebraska's secondary.

After a 13-yard run by James Stewart and a 14-yard pass to Jermaine Chambers, Costa hit Jonathan Harris in stride at Nebraska's 35.

Harris cut inside, faking out cornerback Kareem Moss and safety Tony Veland.

Harris outran everyone else, 44 yards to the end

Brook Berringer relieved starting quarterback Tommie Frazier in the opening quarter, before firing a second-quarter 19-yard scoring pass to tight end Mark Gilman for Nebraska's first points in the Orange Bowl win.

zone. Prewitt added the extra point, giving Miami a 17-7 lead. Miami, however, was penalized for excessive celebration.

The Hurricanes were hurt by excessive penalties—they had seven for 63 yards in the first half—and a third-quarter penalty led to a safety for Nebraska.

Two penalties on a rush by Stewart—an illegal block and a personal foul—gave Miami a second and 20 from its four.

Nebraska defensive tackle Dwayne Harris followed that up by running around tackle Zev Lumelski and hauling Costa down in the back of the end zone for the safety. With 11:35 remaining in the third quarter, Miami's lead was cut to 17-9.

A fumble by Nebraska quarterback Brook Berringer halted what had been a promising drive just before the end of the third quarter. The ball was recovered by UM linebacker James Burgess on Miami's 36, stopping a drive that featured three completions of 13 yards or better.

Miami took a 10-7 lead at halftime after a dominating first quarter and a mistake-filled second. The first-half keys for Miami were Sapp, who made three drive-stopping plays, and quarterback Frank Costa, who completed nine of 17 passes for 153 yards and one touchdown.

Berringer, who replaced starter Frazier after Miami took a 10-0 lead, represented the turning point for Nebraska—even though Berringer completed just

Sophomore I-back sensation Lawrence Phillips clips off yardage against Miami in the 1995 Orange Bowl. Phillips rushed for 96 tough yards against the Hurricanes' No. 1-rated defense in the nation.

THE ORANGE BOWL: NEBRASKA VS. MIAMI

three of six passes for 19 first-half yards.

Miami's first-half touchdown followed an interception by Carlos Jones of a Frazier pass. Sapp clobbered Frazier as he released the ball and Jones' interception gave the Hurricanes possession at the UM three.

Costa has never looked better than he did leading Miami on the 97-yard touchdown drive that followed to end the first quarter. Going into the game, the Hurricanes said they wanted to run to open up the pass.

Instead, Miami passed to open up the run.

After a two-yard run by Stewart, Costa took a three-step drop and threw a quick pass to Trent Jones, who was lined up in the slot. Nebraska linebacker Ed Stewart tried so hard to come up and make a play, he ran right by Jones, who breezed to the end zone for a 35-yard touchdown. Miami had its 10-0 lead with :04 remaining in the quarter.

Touchdown hero Cory Schlesinger looks for an opening in Orange Bowl action against Miami. The Cornhusker fullback scored the tying and winning TDs in the come-from-behind 24-17 win that netted Nebraska the national championship.

148

NEBRASKA'S LONG, WINDING ROAD HAS HAPPY END

By MIKE KLOCKE
Fort Myers (Fla.) News-Press

MIAMI, Jan. 1, 1995—Punt snaps sailed into the ozone. There was a corner kick that would have made any World Cup team from the past summer proud. Fumbles littered the turf. Quarterbacks were flip-flopped in and out of the game.

So it was last night with a national championship at stake in the Orange Bowl.

But it all has to matter so little to Tom Osborne, one of the truly good people in college athletics, who now wears a label he's sought for almost a quarter century.

National champion.

The Orange Bowl was bizarre and not particularly well played.

And you can bet the red-and-white clad fans from Nebraska couldn't care a lick.

Because they'll crawl back into their Winnebagos and head back to Lincoln as the nation's best college football team.

They won because of a tremendous—and courageous—effort by quarterback Tommie Frazier and because of two late touchdown runs by unheralded fullback Cory Schlesinger.

This was sweet corn—24-17. Nothing else matters, including what unbeaten Penn State does Monday in the Rose Bowl.

Nebraska is king.

The wait—a long, sufferable wait—is over. The Osborne legacy had included 218 victories, an .829 winning percentage and a long-standing reputation for class.

It also had included losses in the last three Orange Bowls. Losses in the last seven bowl-game appearances, including six to either Miami or Florida State.

No. 1. At last! Husker players signal what both major polls finally validated: Nebraska is college football's 1994 national champion!

Losses in bowls in 13 of Osborne's 21 previous years.

But after adversity and the Hurricanes had dominated them for three quarters, the Cornhuskers showed their poise and guile.

Schlesinger—whose hobby is driving in demolition derbies—ran up the gut of the Miami defense for as many touchdowns as he's had in the last two years.

Frazier made the key runs and a crucial two-point conversion pass. The defense played in a frenzy.

And the Cornhuskers won at Miami's home field, which had been its personal den of horrors.

There were some crazy moments, including a punt play destined for all blooper films.

With a seemingly comfortable 17-9 lead, Miami long snapper Jeffrey Taylor decided to hike the ball halfway from the Orange Bowl to the Atlantic Ocean.

When Miami punter Dane Prewitt finally ran down the eighth bad punt snap this season, he used his soccer background. Instead of picking up the ball, Prewitt kicked it into the end zone and out of bounds.

The resulting penalty gave Nebraska a surprising chance to get back in the game. But quarterback Brook Berringer promptly had a pass intercepted.

That's when Osborne, who has been roundly criticized for his big-game coaching, made the decision of his career.

Back in went Frazier, the storybook quarterback who hadn't seen regular action since Sept. 24 because of a blood clot in his knee.

Many thought his career was over. Certainly his season had seemed finished. He had been yanked for Berringer after the first quarter.

But he directed two fourth-quarter scoring drives, and ended a legacy of Nebraska failures with championships at stake.

It was strange. It was bizarre. But there's a national championship headed back to Nebraska.

Cornhuskers don't care about style points.

◄·······················

Huskerheads elevate the pre-game pageantry at the Orange Bowl in Miami.

VICTORY CONFIRMS IT: OSBORNE A CHAMPION

By DAN LE BATARD
Miami Herald

MIAMI, Jan. 2, 1995—The tall redhead took his headset off and made the slow walk to the center of the Orange Bowl field at about midnight Sunday. Didn't need directions. Tom Osborne knew the way. For more than a decade, he has seen the faces approaching from the other sideline, and they were always smiling. Howard Schnellenberger. Jimmy Johnson. Bobby Bowden. Dennis Erickson. This time was different, though. This time, Tom Osborne didn't have to give the congratulations to somebody else.

Wins a lot but never when it matters. That has always been Osborne's trophy. He is expected to get a different one when the final polls are released Tuesday, the crystal one that elevates him from merely winner to champion.

He had lost seven consecutive bowl games before Sunday,

Head coach Tom Osborne addresses his players during the 1995 Orange Bowl. It was Osborne's first national championship in 22 years at the Nebraska helm, and the Cornhuskers' first win in their last six Orange Bowl appearances.

had a 1-10 record in his past 11 games against Top 10 teams. Sunday changed everything about his career.

When Osborne walked into his news conference after Sunday's 24-17 victory over the University of Miami, there were two trophies at the podium—a big one filled with oranges and a small one. Osborne looked at the big one and said, "I didn't know this actually existed." He pointed to the small one and said, "I used to collect these."

Osborne is the type of guy you root for, which is why as time ticked away Sunday, you saw as odd a sight as you'll see in sports: one minute left in a live game and referee came over to the sideline, just to shake Osborne's hand.

"This is the greatest moment of my life because nobody deserves it more than Tom Osborne," said offensive lineman Zach Wiegert, whose team, after falling behind 17-7, held Miami to minus 37 yards in the fourth quarter. "The man perseveres, and we persevered tonight. This one is special."

Osborne's personality is every bit as pale as his face, as dull as dedication. Before Sunday's game, in a tunnel filled with testosterone, his players banged helmets and flexed. "They can't touch us," one yelled. "Dogfight all night, baby," shouted another. Osborne stood behind them, expression never changing, chewing gum and looking at his watch. His players sprinted out but Osborne walked calmly behind them, past UM Coach Dennis Erickson, who already was so wired that his shirt was disheveled and his baseball cap was crooked.

When fullback Cory Schlesinger scored the winning touchdown with 2:46 remaining, Osborne did not celebrate. He turned around and pushed his frolicking players back, somehow keeping control amid chaos. He is pretty constant that way, on the field and in life. He has been running three miles a day for three decades, around the same Nebraska track. The critics, before Sunday, said it was a metaphor for his career: Always running but going nowhere.

But he remains one of college football's last good guys, standing above a sport that now has more to do with sneaker scandals than pep rallies. He doesn't drink, doesn't smoke, says nothing spicier than dadgummit. He is a Sunday school teacher who has campaigned against pornography, a vegetarian who weights the same 193 pounds he weighed in college. He is saddened because he has been home for only one Christmas in the past 22 years, which might explain why he sat alone in a 1,000-seat ballroom a few years ago, humming Christmas carols to himself.

"To win a national championship, you've got to have a little luck," friend Joe Paterno, Penn State coach, said earlier this year, "and Tom has had no luck at all."

He had some Sunday: A snap sailing over the head of Miami punter Dane Prewitt. A two-point conversion that didn't get caught by Nebraska tight end Eric Alford as much as it stuck to his chest. A pass for Miami wide receiver Taj Johnson, breaking free 20 yards behind the defense, flying over his hands instead.

So when Sunday was done, the scoreboard lights did not lie. They said Osborne was a winner, finally.

It was a touch redundant. We've known that all along.

FRAZIER IS MVP AFTER SHAKY START

By SUSAN MILLER DEGNAN
Miami Herald

Tommie Frazier was right. What mattered most to the University of Nebraska in Sunday's FedEx Orange Bowl was who finished, not who started.

And it was him.

Tommie Frazier: Orange Bowl MVP and fourth-quarter redeemer in Nebraska's 24-17 victory and first national championship since 1971.

With one fourth-quarter two-point conversion toss to tight end Eric Alford—who cut left to right into the end zone—and a 25-yard weave down the middle to set up a 14-yard touchdown run by fullback Cory Schlesinger with 2:46 left, Frazier deftly turned around a not-so-memorable start.

"There is life, and there is athletics. But this is the highest I've ever reached in either," said Frazier, a junior who sat out the final eight regular-season games because of blood clots behind his right knee. "There is no doubt we are national champions. No doubt. We beat Miami at Miami."

Tommie Frazier looks downfield in the fourth-quarter frenzy of the Orange Bowl. Frazier's two-point conversion pass to Eric Alford tied the game at 17-17.

Frazier's numbers Sunday: three for five passing with one interception for 25 yards. He ran seven times for 31 yards—the most important the 25-yard sprint with about five minutes remaining.

Brook Berringer, who took over for Frazier at the beginning of the second quarter and went out with 11:59 remaining, had these numbers: eight completions in 15 attempts with one interception for an 81-yard passing total—including a 19-yard touchdown pass. Berringer lost four yards rushing on seven carries.

"We both contributed to this victory," Berringer said of Frazier and himself. "We wanted this so badly."

Breaking the Streak

Nebraska ended a seven-game losing streak in bowls.

'88 Fiesta Bowl.............Florida State 31, Nebraska 28

'89 Orange Bowl........................Miami 23, Nebraska 3

'90 Fiesta Bowl..............Florida State 41, Nebraska 17

'91 Citrus Bowl............Georgia Tech 45, Nebraska 21

'92 Orange Bowl......................Miami 22, Nebraska 0

'93 Orange Bowl..........Florida State 27, Nebraska 14

'94 Orange Bowl..........Florida State 18, Nebraska 16

'95 Orange Bowl.....................Nebraska 24, Miami 17

OB BECOMES HUSKERS' TURF

By DAVID J. NEAL
Miami Herald

MIAMI, Jan. 1, 1995—Nebraska defensive tackle Christian Peter kicked at one spot of the Orange Bowl turf furiously. Again and again, he kicked at the growing divot as cameras clicked and fans howled.

Finally, the tuft of turf was big enough for Peter to scoop up and slam on top of his head as teammate Joel Wilks shouted, "Plant that in your yard!"

It was appropriate because at that moment, the northwest corner of the Orange Bowl was a little part of Nebraska.

Minutes after they had secured the national championship they had waited 23 years for, the Cornhuskers decided to share the moment. They marched back out of their locker room and joined their fans, who have seen them lose seven consecutive bowl games and get beaten the previous three times they had played the University of Miami in the Orange Bowl.

"We all decided to come back on the field because they've traveled really far to watch us play and have always stuck with us," right guard Brenden Stai said.

Stai gasped, "It's something . . . remarkable . . . it's hard to explain. My class is going to go down in history."

Said Cory Schlesinger, who scored the Cornhuskers' final two touchdowns: "This is great to come back here to win it in here . . . it's amazing, it's beautiful."

Meanwhile, Peter was jumping on Wilks, players were flipping used equipment into the stands to the delirious faithful, and every Nebraska player with dirty jerseys and pants was being assaulted by a frantic media corps.

"We got the monkey off our backs," Peter shouted. "We got Miami in Miami—case closed."

No. 1 Nebraska 24
No. 3 Miami 17

Nebraska......0 7 2 15 — 24
Miami..........10 0 7 0 — 17

Mia—FG Prewitt 44
Mia—T. Jones 35 pass from Costa (Prewitt kick)
Neb—Gilman 19 pass from Berringer (Erstad kick)
Mia—J. Harris 44 pass from Costa (Prewitt kick)
Neb—Safety, Costa sacked by D. Harris in end zone
Neb—Schlesinger 15 run (Frazier pass to Alford)
Neb—Schlesinger 14 run (Sieler kick)
A—81,753.

TEAM STATISTICS

Category	Neb	Mia
First downs	20	14
Rushes-yards	46-199	28-29
Passing yards	106	248
Return yards	17	(-6)
Passes	11-20-2	18-35-1
Punts	7-41	7-40
Fumbles-lost	2-1	2-0
Penalties-yards	3-20	11-92
Time of possession	32:32	27:28

INDIVIDUAL STATISTICS

RUSHING: Nebraska—Phillips 19-96, Schlesinger 6-48, Frazier 7-31, Benning 3-18, Washington 1-9, Childs 3-1, Berringer 7-(minus 4). Miami—J. Stewart 17-72, J. Harris 1-6, L. Jones 1-2, Ferguson 2-1, Costa 6-(minus 17), Prewitt 1-(minus 35).

PASSING: Nebraska—Frazier 3-5-1-25, Berringer 8-15-1-81. Miami—Costa 18-35-1-248.

RECEIVING: Nebraska—Muhammad 4-60, Phillips 4-13, Gilman 1-19, Holbein 1-7, Baul 1-7. Miami—C.T. Jones 6-63, German 3-22, Tellison 2-53, Wimberly 2-18, J. Harris 1-44, T. Jones 1-35, Chambers 1-14, Ferguson 1-3, Y. Green 1-(minus 4).

THE 1994 NATIONAL CHAMPIONS

THE 1994 NATIONAL CHAMPION NEBRASKA CORNHUSKERS

FINAL POLLS

ASSOCIATED PRESS TOP 25

	Team	Rec.	Votes	LW
1.	Nebraska (51 1/2)	13-0-0	1,539 1/2	1
2.	Penn St. (10 1/2)	12-0-0	1,497 1/2	2
3.	Colorado	11-1-0	1,410	4
4.	Florida State	10-1-1	1,320	7
5.	Alabama	12-1-0	1,312	6
6.	Miami (Fla.)	10-2-0	1,249	3
7.	Florida	10-2-1	1,153	5
8.	Texas A&M	10-1-1	1,117	8
9.	Auburn	9-1-1	1,110	9
10.	Utah	10-2-0	955	14
11.	Oregon	9-4-0	810	12
12.	Michigan	8-4-0	732	20
13.	Southern Cal	8-3-1	691	21
14.	Ohio State	9-4-0	672	13
15.	Virginia	9-3-0	648	18
16.	Colorado St.	10-2-0	630	10
17.	North Carolina St.	9-3-0	511	23
18.	Brigham Young	10-3-0	500	22
19.	Kansas St.	9-3-0	496	11
20.	Arizona	8-4-0	364	15
21.	Washington St.	8-4-0	344	24
22.	Tennessee	8-4-0	303	NR
23.	Boston College	7-4-1	236	NR
24.	Mississippi St.	8-4-0	160	16
25.	Texas	8-4-0	90	NR

USA TODAY/CNN TOP 25

	Team	Rec.	Votes	LW
1.	Nebraska (54)	13-0-0	1,542	1
2.	Penn St. (8)	12-0-0	1,496	2
3.	Colorado	11-1-0	1,387	5
4.	Alabama	12-1-0	1,345	6
5.	Florida State	10-1-1	1,325	7
6.	Miami (Fla.)	10-2-0	1,231	3
7.	Florida	10-2-1	1,182	4
8.	Utah	10-2-0	1,034	12
9.	Ohio State	9-4-0	846	11
10.	Brigham Young	10-3-0	840	19
11.	Oregon	9-4-0	834	9
12.	Michigan	8-4-0	797	18
13.	Virginia	9-3-0	777	16
14.	Colorado St.	10-2-0	690	10
15.	Southern Cal	8-3-1	670	22
16.	Kansas St.	9-3-0	657	8
17.	North Carolina St.	9-3-0	627	20
18.	Tennessee	8-4-0	517	24
19.	Washington St.	8-4-0	453	23
20.	Arizona	8-4-0	402	13
21.	North Carolina	8-4-0	312	14
22.	Boston College	7-4-1	301	25
23.	Texas	8-4-0	250	NR
24.	Virginia Tech	8-4-0	188	15
25.	Mississippi St.	8-4-0	149	17

NEBRASKA ALPHABETICAL ROSTER

No.	Name	Pos.	Ht.	Wt.	Yr.	Hometown (High School/College)
47	Aden, Matt	SLB	6-2	200	Fr.	Omaha, Neb. (Northwest)
48	Alderman, Dave	Rover	5-10	180	So.	Omaha, Neb. (North)
36	Alexander, Leonard	MLB	6-1	235	Sr.	Detroit, Mich (Lutheran East)
88	*Alford, Eric	TE	6-2	225	Sr.	Highpoint, N.C. (Central/Gar. City, Kan. CC)
82	Allen, Jacques	WB	6-2	200	Jr.	Kansas City, Mo. (Raytown)
70	Anderson, Eric	OT	6-4	295	Fr.	Lincoln, Neb (Southwest)
23	Arnold, Larry	SLB	6-4	220	So.	Copley, Ohio
7	*Baul, Reggie	SE	5-8	170	Jr.	Bellevue, Neb. (Papillion-LaVista)
21	*Benning, Damon	IB	5-11	205	So.	Omaha, Neb. (Northwest)
18	**Berringer, Brook	QB	6-4	210	Jr.	Goodland, Kan.
#11	Blahak, Chad	LCB	5-10	190	So.	Lincoln, Neb.
20	Booker, Michael	RCB	6-2	200	So.	Oceanside, Calif. (El Camino)
45	*Brown, Clint	SLB	6-1	215	Sr.	Arlington, Neb.
81	Brown, Lance	WB	5-11	180	Fr.	Papillion, Neb. (Papillion-LaVista)
62	Butler, Ted	OL	6-1	240	Fr.	Lincoln, Neb. (Southeast)
90	Carpenter, Tim	TE	6-2	225	Fr.	Columbus, Neb.
61	*Caskey, Brady	OT	6-4	290	Sr.	Stanton, Neb.
26	*Childs, Clinton	IB	6-0	215	Jr.	Omaha, Neb. (North)
#9	Christo, Monte	QB	5-11	175	Fr.	Kearney, Neb.
46	**Colman, Doug	MLB	6-3	240	Jr.	Ventnor, N.J. (Ocean City)
99	***Connealy, Terry	DT	6-5	275	Sr.	Hyannis, Neb.
17	Davenport, Scott	IB	5-6	190	Sr.	Rye Brook, N.Y. (Port Chester)
83	Davis, Aaron	SE	5-11	180	So.	Lincoln, Neb.
2	Dennis, Leslie	RCB	5-8	165	Fr.	Bradenton, Fla. (Southeast)
75	*Dishman, Chris	OT	6-3	305	So.	Cozad, Neb.
4	***Dumas, Troy	SLB	6-4	220	Sr.	Cheyenne, Wyo. (East)
41	**Ellis, Phil	MLB	6-2	225	Jr.	Grand Island, Neb.
6	Erstad, Darin	P/PK	6-2	195	So.	Jamestown, N.D.
15	**Frazier, Tommie	QB	6-2	205	Jr.	Bradenton, Fla. (Manatee)
87	**Gilman, Mark	TE	6-3	240	Jr.	Kalispell, Mont. (Flathead)
54	**Graham, Aaron	C	6-4	280	Jr.	Denton, Texas
58	**Hardin, Luther	OLB	6-2	230	Jr.	O'Fallon, Ill. (Althoff Catholic)
86	**Harris, Dwayne	OLB	6-2	225	Sr.	Bessemer, Ala. (Jess Lanier)
59	Heskew, Josh	C	6-3	250	Fr.	Yukon, Okla (Mustang)
44	Hesse, Jon	MLB	6-4	225	So.	Lincoln, Neb. (Southeast)
92	**Higman, Jerad	OLB	6-1	230	Sr.	Akron, Iowa (Akron-Westfield)
5	*Holbein, Brendan	SE	5-9	180	So.	Cozad, Neh.
62	Hoskinson, Matt	OG	6-1	275	Fr.	Battle Creek, Neb.
51	**Humphrey, Bill	C	6-2	265	Sr.	Libertyville, Ill.
84	Jackson, Sheldon	Rec.	6-3	205	Fr.	Diamond Bar, Calif. (Damien)
34	Jackson, Vershan	FB	6-0	225	Fr.	Omaha, Neb. (South)
96	Jenkins, Jason	DT	6-5	265	Jr.	Hammonton, N.J. (Oakcrest/Dodge City CC)
33	*Johnson, Clester	WB	5-11	210	Jr.	Bellevue, Neb. (West)
84	***Jones, Donta	OLB	6-2	220	Sr.	LaPlata, Md. (Pomfret McDonough)
19	Kosch, Jesse	P	6-0	180	Fr.	Columbus, Neb. (Scotus)
30	Knuckles, Brian	IB	5-11	195	Jr.	Charlotte, N.C. (West/Coffeyville, Kan. CC)
89	Lake, Jeff	SE	6-4	205	Fr.	Columbus, Neb. (Lakeview)
79	Lesser, Mike	OG	6-4	265	Fr.	Pierce, Neb.
#2	Livingston, John	SE	6-0	170	Jr.	San Marcos, Calif. (Hemet/Palomar CC/ASU)
22	**Makovicka, Jeff	FB	5-10	210	Jr.	Brainard, Neb. (East Butler)

THE 1994 NATIONAL CHAMPIONS

No.	Name	Pos.	Ht.	Wt.	Yr.	Hometown (School)
49	Martin, John	OLB	6-2	245	Sr.	Wahoo, Neb. (Neumann)
#5	McFarlin, Octavious	Rover	6-0	180	Fr.	Bastrop, Texas
78	Mikos, Kory	OT	6-5	260	So.	Seward, Neb.
14	**Miles, Barron	LCB	5-8	165	Sr.	Roselle, N.J. (Abraham Clark)
10	*Minter, Mike	FS	5-10	175	So.	Lawton, Okla.
42	Morrow, Ed	OLB	6-4	230	So.	Ferguson, Mo. (St. Louis McCluer)
29	**Moss, Kareem	Rover	5-10	190	Sr.	Spartanburg, S.C. (Garden City CC)
27	***Muhammad, Abdul	WB	5-9	160	Sr.	Compton, Calif. (Carson)
38	Norris, Chris	FB	5-10	235	Jr.	Papillion, Neb. (Papillion-LaVista)
43	Noster, Sean	SLB	6-3	215	Fr.	San Antonio, Texas (John Marshall)
63	Nunns, Brian	OT	6-2	280	Jr.	Lincoln, Neb.
97	Ogard, Jeff	DT	6-6	290	So.	St. Paul, Neb.
69	**Ott, Steve	OG	6-4	275	Jr.	Henderson, Neb.
52	**Penland, Aaron	WLB	6-1	215	Jr.	Jacksonville, Fla. (University Christian)
57	**Pesterfield, Jason	DT	6-3	260	Sr.	Pauls Valley, Okla.
55	*Peter, Christian	DT	6-2	285	Jr.	Locust, N.J. (Middletown South)
95	Peter, Jason	DT	6-4	275	Fr.	Locust, N.J. (Milford Academy)
1	*Phillips, Lawrence	IB	6-0	200	So.	West Covina, Calif. (Baldwin Park)
73	Pollack, Fred	OT	6-4	305	Fr.	Omaha, Neb. (Creighton Prep)
80	**Popplewell, Brett	SE	6-0	205	Jr.	Melbourne, Australia (Carey Grammar)
65	*Pruitt, Bryan	OG	6-1	255	Sr.	Midlothian, Ill. (St. Laurence)
13	Retzlaff, Ted	PK	5-11	180	Fr.	Waverly, Neb.
39	Roberts, Mike	Rover	6-1	175	So.	Omaha, Neb. (Central)
35	Sakalosky, Jeff	WLB	5-11	210	Fr.	Omaha, Neb. (Gross)
74	Saltsman, Scott	DT	6-2	255	So.	Wichita Falls, Texas (Rider)
40	**Schlesinger, Cory	FB	6-0	230	Sr.	Duncan, Neb. (Columbus)
37	*Schmadeke, Darren	LCB	5-8	180	Jr.	Albion, Neb.
28	Schuster, Brian	FB	5-11	210	So.	Fullerton, Neb.
85	**Shaw, Matt	TE	6-3	235	Sr.	Lincoln, Neb. (Northeast)
12	***Sieler, Tom	PK	6-5	205	Sr.	Las Vegas, Nev. (Chaparral)
66	***Stai, Brenden	OG	6-5	300	Sr.	Yorba Linda, Calif. (Anaheim Esperanza)
31	Stanley, Chad	FB	5-11	215	Jr.	Lebanon, Kan. (Smith-Center)
32	***Stewart, Ed	WLB	6-1	220	Sr.	Chicago, Ill. (Mount Carmel)
16	*Stokes, Eric	FS	5-11	175	So.	Lincoln, Neb. (East)
67	Taylor, Aaron	OG	6-1	290	Fr.	Wichita Falls, Texas (Rider)
91	*Terwilliger, Ryan	WLB	6-5	220	So.	Grant, Neb.
93	Tomich, Jared	OLB	6-2	250	So.	St. John, Ind. (Lake Central)
94	Townsend, Larry	DT	6-4	285	So.	San Jose, Calif. (Yerba Buena)
77	Treu, Adam	OT	6-6	290	So.	Lincoln, Neb. (Pius X)
11	Turman, Matt	QB	5-11	165	So.	Wahoo, Neb. (Neumann)
24	Uhlir, Todd	IB	5-10	210	Fr.	Battle Creek, Neb.
71	Van Cleave, Mike	OG	6-2	270	Fr.	Huffman, Texas (Hargrave)
25	Vedral, Jon	WB	5-11	195	So.	Gregory, S.D.
9	**Veland, Tony	FS	6-2	200	Jr.	Omaha, Neb. (Benson)
68	Volin, Steve	OG	6-2	275	Jr.	Wahoo, Neb.
53	Vrzal, Matt	C	6-1	290	So.	Grand Island, Neb.
3	*Washington, Riley	SE	5-9	170	So.	Chula Vista, Calif. (San Diego SW)
72	***Wiegert, Zach	OT	6-5	300	Sr.	Fremont, Neb. (Bergan)
76	**Wilks, Joel	OG	6-3	280	Sr.	Hastings, Neb.
#28	Williams, Jamel	WLB	6-2	195	So.	Merrillville, Ind.
8	*Williams, Tyrone	RCB	6-0	185	Jr.	Palmetto, Fla. (Manatee)
85	Wistrom, Grant	OLB	6-5	230	Fr.	Webb City, Mo.
#22	Wrice, Trampis	RCB	5-9	170	So.	Valdosta, Ga.
64	Zatechka, Jon	OG	6-2	280	Fr.	Lincoln, Neb. (East)
56	***Zatechka, Rob	OT	6-5	315	Sr.	Lincoln, Neb. (East)

1994 NEBRASKA FOOTBALL STATISTICS (REGULAR SEASON)

RESULTS

DATE	OPPONENT	SCORE	RECORD
Aug. 28	West Virginia @	31-0	(1-0)
Sept. 8	Texas Tech *	42-16	(2-0)
Sept. 17	UCLA *	49-21	(3-0)
Sept. 24	Pacific *	70-21	(4-0)
Oct. 1	Wyoming *	42-32	(5-0)
Oct. 8	Oklahoma State *	32-3	(6-0)
Oct. 15	Kansas State	17-6	(7-0)
Oct. 22	Missouri	42-7	(8-0)
Oct. 29	Colorado *	24-7	(9-0)
Nov. 5	Kansas *	45-17	(10-0)
Nov. 12	Iowa State	28-12	(11-0)
Nov. 25	Oklahoma	13-3	(12-0)
Jan. 1	Miami #	24-17	(13-0)

* Home   @ East Rutherford, N.J.   # Orange Bowl
Home: 6-0   Away: 7-0   Big Eight: 7-0

CATEGORY	NU	OPP.
First Downs	293	176
Rushing Attempts	687	401
Rushing Yards Gained	4356	1359
Rushing Yards Lost	276	408
NET RUSHING YARDS	4080	951
Yards Per Rush	5.9	2.4
Rushing Yards Per Game	340.0	79.3
Passes Attempted	210	364
Passes Completed	120	172
Passes Had Intercepted	7	17
Pass Completion Percentage	.571	.473
NET YARDS PASSING	1654	2155
Yards Per Pass Attempt	7.9	5.9
Yards Per Pass Completion	13.8	12.5
Passing Yards Per Game	137.8	174.6
Total Plays	897	765
Total Plays Per Game	74.8	63.0
TOTAL NET YARDS	5734	3106
Yards Gained Per Play	6.4	4.2
Yards Gained Per Game	477.0	258.0
Kickoff Return Yards	571	636
Average Yardage Per Kickoff Return	22.8	10.2
Punt Return Yards	419	69
Average Yardage Per Punt Return	8.6	2.9
Interception Return Yards	218	34
Average Yardage Per Interception Return	12.8	4.9
Average Yards Per Punt	(50) 42.6	(88) 41.4
Fumbles Lost	13	4
Yard Penalized	(76) 670	(60) 475

INDIVIDUAL

RUSHING	Att	Gain	Loss	Net	YPA	YPG	TD	LG
Phillips	286	1785	63	1722	6.0	143.5	16	74
Schlesinger	63	459	3	456	7.2	38.0	4	41
Childs	62	399	4	395	6.4	32.9	5	30
Benning	67	376	9	367	5.5	30.6	5	23
Makovicka	47	321	0	321	6.8	26.8	2	50
Berringer	71	409	130	279	3.9	23.3	6	28
Frazier	33	276	28	248	7.5	62.0	6	58
Schuster	13	99	1	96	7.5	8.2	0	33
Turman	19	94	14	80	4.2	7.3	0	24
Muhammad	5	39	7	32	6.4	2.7	0	30
Uhlir	6	27	0	27	4.5	5.4	0	10
Davenport	4	27	2	25	6.3	8.3	0	12
Alford	1	17	0	17	17.0	1.6	0	17
Jackson	3	12	0	12	4.0	4.0	0	8
Norris	2	7	0	7	3.5	2.3	0	5
Washington	1	5	0	5	5.0	.5	0	5
Kucera	1	4	0	4	4.0	4.0	0	4
Stanley	1	0	0	0	.0	.0	0	0
Held	1	0	0	0	.0	.0	0	0
Team	1	0	15	-15	-15.0	15.0	0	0
NEB.	687	4350	276	4080	5.9	340.0	44	
OPP.	401	1359	408	951	2.4	79.3	8	

PASSING	Att	Cmp	Pct	Int	Yds	Att	Cmp	Game	TD	Pass
Berringer	151	94	.623	5	1295	8.6	13.8	107.9	10	64
Frazier	44	19	.432	2	272	6.2	14.4	68.3	4	35
Turman	12	6	.500	0	81	6.8	13.5	7.4	1	24
Vedral	1	1	1.000	0	5	5.0	5.0	.4	0	0
Phillips	1	0	.000	0	0	.0	.0	.0	0	0
Kucera	1	0	.000	0	0	.0	.0	.0	0	0
NEB.	210	120	.571	7	1654	7.9	13.0	137.5	15	
OPP.	360	172	.473	17	2155	5.9	12.5	179.6	10	

RECEIVING	Recpts	Yds	YPR	YPG	TD	Long
Muhammad	23	360	16.7	30.0	2	44
Phillips	22	172	7.8	14.3	0	27
Baul	17	300	17.7	25.0	3	51
Gilman	17	196	11.5	16.3	1	48
Alford	14	271	19.4	24.6	4	46
Holbein	9	88	9.0	7.3	2	30
Benning	5	68	13.6	5.7	0	37
Childs	5	50	11.6	4.8	0	26
Johnson	4	93	23.3	7.8	2	64
Makovicka	1	5	5.0	.4	0	5
Vedral	1	7	7.0	.6	0	7
Carpenter	1	12	12.0	1.5	0	12
Lake	1	24	24.0	4.8	1	24
NEB.	120	1654	13.8	137.8	15	
OPP.	172	2156	12.5	179.6	10	

THE 1994 NATIONAL CHAMPIONS

PUNT RETURNS	Returns	Yds	YPR	YPG	TD	Long
Moss	31	234	7.6	15.5	0	28
Baul	11	119	10.8	9.9	0	22
Williams	4	42	10.5	3.8	0	18
Miles	1	21	21.0	1.8	0	21
Wrice	1	0	.0	.0	0	0
Childs	1	3	3.0	.3	0	2
NEB.	49	419	8.6	34.9	0	
OPP.	24	69	2.9	5.8	0	

KICKOFF RETURNS	Returns	Yds	YPR	YPG	TD	Long
Benning	12	308	25.7	25.7	0	54
Childs	9	190	21.1	15.8	0	34
Makovicka	1	10	10.0	.8	0	10
Uhlir	1	30	30.0	6.0	0	30
Schlesinger	1	16	16.0	1.3	0	14
Williams	1	17	17.0	1.7	0	17
NEB.	25	571	22.8	47.6	0	
OPP.	35	636	18.2	53.0	0	

PUNTING	Punts	Yds	YPP	PPG	Long
Erstad	50	2130	42.6	4.2	73
NEB.	50	2130	42.6	4.2	
OPP.	88	3645	41.4	7.3	

SCORING	Pass Rec	Rush	K	Pass Rec	Run	FG	Pts
Phillips	0	16	0	0	0	0	96
Sieler	0	0	40	0	0	4	52
Frazier	0	6	0	0	2	0	40
Berringer	0	6	0	0	0	0	36
Benning	0	5	0	0	0	0	30
Childs	0	5	0	0	0	0	30
Alford	4	0	0	1	0	0	26
Schlesinger	0	4	0	0	0	0	24
Erstad	0	0	10	1	0	3	21
Baul	3	0	0	0	0	0	18
Holbein	2	0	0	0	0	0	12
Makovicka	0	2	0	0	0	0	12
Muhammad	2	0	0	0	0	0	12
Johnson	2	0	0	0	0	0	12
Gilman	1	0	0	0	0	0	6
Lake	1	0	0	0	0	0	6
Retzlaff	0	0	2	0	0	0	2
NEB.	16	44	52	2	2	7	435
OPP.	10	0	14	1	0	7	145

INTERCEPTIONS	Intcpts	Yds	YPR	TD	Long
Miles	5	25	7.0	0	27
Williams	3	34	11.3	0	28
Veland	3	35	11.7	0	35
Moss	2	0	.0	0	0
Dennis	1	48	48.0	0	48
Collins	1	8	8.0	0	8
Dumas	1	54	54.0	0	54
Brown	1	4	4.0	0	4
NEB.	17	318	12.8	0	
OPP.	7	34	4.5	0	

DEFENSE	UT	TT	AT	Sack/YDS	TL/Yds	FF	FR	BLO	PD	Int
Stewart	41	96	55	3.5/8	5.5/23	0	1	0	1	0
Peter	32	71	39	7/31	14/45	0	0	0	2	0
Dumas	38	69	31	1/6	4/17	1	0	0	0	1
Moss	41	66	25	2/12	2/13	0	0	0	4	2
Ellis	24	58	34	0.5/2	7.5/21	0	0	0	0	0
Jones	23	52	29	5/31	10/52	1	0	0	2	0
Colman	17	51	34	2/15	3/16	1	1	0	1	0
Harris	15	43	28	5/38	10/45	1	0	0	4	0
Connealy	13	42	29	6.5/37	7.5/38	1	0	0	0	0
Miles	24	40	16	0/0	0/0	1	0	4	13	5
Williams	31	38	7	0/0	0/0	0	0	0	5	3
Stokes	12	36	24	0/0	0/0	0	0	0	2	0
Wistrom	14	36	22	4.5/49	6.5/55	0	0	0	0	0
Veland	13	26	13	0/0	0/0	0	0	0	1	3
Tomich	12	23	11	1/7	4/15	0	0	0	0	0
Terwilliger	8	19	11	2/8	3/14	0	0	0	0	0
Brown	8	18	10	0/0	1/1	0	1	0	0	1
Dennis	9	16	7	0/0	0/0	0	0	0	3	1
Pesterfield	9	15	6	3/26	5/33	0	0	0	1	0
McFarlin	6	15	9	0/0	0/0	0	0	0	1	0
Vedral	6	11	5	0/0	0/0	0	0	0	0	0
Hesse	5	11	6	0/0	2/2	0	0	0	0	0
Schmadeke	8	9	1	0/0	0/0	0	0	0	1	0
Penland	2	9	7	0/0	0/0	0	0	0	0	0
Hardin	4	9	5	0/0	0/0	0	0	0	0	0
Alexander	2	8	6	0/0	0/0	0	0	0	0	0
Saltsman	2	8	6	0/0	1/1	0	0	0	0	0
Peter	2	8	6	0/0	1/3	0	0	0	2	0
Minter	3	7	4	0/0	1/1	0	0	0	1	0
Townsend	2	6	4	0/0	1/3	0	0	0	0	0
Williams	5	6	1	0/0	0/0	0	0	0	0	0
Noster	3	5	2	0/0	0/0	0	0	0	0	0
Wrice	2	5	3	0/0	0/0	0	0	1	0	0
Arnold	1	4	3	0/0	0/0	0	0	0	0	0
Benning	1	4	3	0/0	0/0	0	1	0	0	0
Erstad	2	4	2	0/0	0/0	0	0	0	0	0
Higman	1	3	4	0/0	0/0	0	0	0	0	0
Aden	1	4	3	0/0	0/0	0	0	0	0	0
Booker	2	4	2	0/0	0/0	0	0	0	0	0
Makovicka	1	1	2	0/0	0/0	0	0	0	0	0
Childs	1	3	2	0/0	0/0	0	0	0	0	0
Ogard	1	3	2	0/0	1/1	0	0	0	0	0
Collins	0	2	2	0/0	0/0	0	0	0	1	1
Jenkins	0	2	2	0/0	0/0	0	0	0	0	0
Sakalosky	0	2	2	0/0	0/0	0	0	0	0	0
Morrow	0	2	2	0/0	0/0	0	0	0	0	0
Retzlaff	2	2	2	0/0	0/0	0	0	0	0	0
Pruitt	2	2	0	0/0	0/0	0	0	0	0	0
Popplewell	1	1	0	0/0	0/0	0	0	0	0	0
Sieler	0	1	1	0/0	0/0	0	0	0	0	0
Muhammad	1	1	0	0/0	0/0	0	0	0	0	0
Blahak	1	1	0	0/0	0/0	0	0	0	1	0
Schlesinger	1	1	0	0/0	0/0	0	0	0	0	0
Winder	0	1	1	0/0	0/0	0	0	0	0	0
Card	0	1	1	0/0	0/0	0	0	0	0	0
Schuster	0	1	1	0/0	0/0	0	0	0	0	0
	455	530	985	43/280	91/402	6	4	5	46	17